Here's what industry leaders are

"Data is the new currency that will drive business and regulatory compliance strategy. The root cause of many company ailments is how data is managed. Jay does a great job highlighting the techniques and approaches to solve complex problems and achieve corporate strategies in the age of data."

Ray Vazquez,
CEO, Infinitive Insight

"Corporate data initiatives fail because the technical team is unable to communicate clearly the business value that can be derived from harnessing the power of their data. In his book, Jay has done a great job of bridging the IT/Business gap by breaking through the technical jargon and clearly articulating the business case for investment in data as a corporate asset. This is crucial for both competitive advantage, as well as, ensuring compliance in today's highly regulated environment."

Kathy Keller,
Managing Director, Newbold Advisors, LLC

"Data-driven leaders must empower their teams to deliver on the business's need for near real time analytics across small and big data. In Data-Driven Leaders Always Win, Jay Zaidi makes a case for investing in foundational capabilities like a data catalog, master data management, data quality, and data governance. The emergence of new self-service data tools and approaches is making it possible for everyone in the enterprise to leverage data, to make better decisions, and achieve better business outcomes."

Alex Gorelik,
CEO, Waterline Data

"In his aptly named book, Jay Zaidi makes the basic argument that being 'Data-Driven' has less to do with having a lot of big data and more to do with understanding and analyzing the context around the data you have. Jay thoughtfully explains that data, like any other form of information, cannot be taken at face value and that being 'Data-Driven' isn't just about cycling data though your organization; it's about making sure that people are able to both quickly find the right data and place that data in the appropriate context."

Satyen Sangani,
Co-founder and CEO, Alation

"Data-driven organizations aim for frictionless data processing to significantly reduce time-to-value. In Data-Driven Leaders Always Win, Jay highlights the fact that IT and Business teams can achieve their common goals by utilizing new technology, and refining their data management processes."

Adam Wilson,
CEO, Trifacta

"Today, every organization is in the data business, and every business needs data-driven leaders. This book introduces you to the most important and demanding areas of information management and provides practical insight into how you can use data to rapidly rise and ultimately win."

Greg Steffine,
BI Strategist and Award-Winning Author

"According to Alibaba's Jack Ma, data will become the biggest production material in the future, it will become a public resource like water, electricity and oil. This has resulted in a paradigm shift in data management. In this timely and insightful book, Jay has done an excellent job outlining the business case and presenting practical steps to help leaders develop a data culture within their organizations."

Samra Sulaiman,
Founder, ConsultData LLC

You'll Benefit from This Book If You Follow These Simple Rules!

- Read each chapter and the "Key Takeaways and Action Items" that follow. As you read, stop and ask yourself how you can apply the key takeaways and actions items.

- Make some notes after the last page of each chapter, and use them as ticklers for when you discuss the ideas and concepts with others.

- Read all chapters within a particular "Part" in sequential order, since they are interrelated. You may read the "Parts" in random order.

- Underline important points as you read.

- Make notes on the back of the book to capture what works and what doesn't and how you have overcome adversity. You can use these notes to provide a readout to your management team or peers.

- Influencing organizational change is very hard, so never forget the quote by Mahatma Gandhi: *"Be the change you wish to see in the world."*

DATA-DRIVEN LEADERS ALWAYS WIN

Der Suri,

Hope you enjoy reading my
book, after all it's all
about 'DATA'.

Best.
Jay Zaidi
Sept - 2016

DATA-DRIVEN LEADERS ALWAYS WIN

THE ESSENTIAL GUIDE FOR LEADERS IN THE AGE OF DATA

JAY ZAIDI

Foreword by Dr. Kirk Borne

 AlyData

2016

Data-Driven Leaders Always Win

by Jay Zaidi

July 2016 First Edition
Revision History for the First Edition:
2016-07-01: First release

Use of the information and instructions contained in this work is at your own risk.

ISBN: 0-692-72008-1
ISBN 13: 978-0-69272-008-0
Library of Congress Control Number: 2016908523
Cover Concept: Jay Zaidi
Cover Design: Ratnesh Singh
Print layout/formatting: Slaven Kovačević
Author's Profile Photo: Ali Rizvi Photography

DEDICATION

This work is dedicated to
my parents, Ali Akhtar and Nuzhat;
my wife, Shabnam;
my children, Ali, Mariam, and Reza;

and

to my trusted MacBook Pro,
which has been my steady companion
throughout this amazing journey!
It kept me company on many a sleepless night.

Contents

PART THREE

Perils of Not Investing in Strategic Data Management

PART FOUR

Who's Leading Your Data Function?

PART FIVE

Dealing with Data Management Challenges

PART SIX

Building a Data-Driven Company

PART SEVEN

Demystifying Data Management

PART EIGHT

Take Steps to Win with Data

APPENDIX

FOREWORD BY DR. KIRK BORNE

In the beginning was data. How do we know this? Because many (if not all) creation stories from all cultures were essentially developed as an explanation of the world as observed by humans. Whether it was the great flood, or mysterious eclipses of the sun, or seasonal changes, or the diversity of life forms, or the existence of diverse substances (earth, fire, wind, and water), or any number of other observed facts, in all of these cases, human societies used stories to explain the evidence that was presented before them. Though the early interpretations of the evidence (i.e., the data) were not exactly scientific, the process was scientific based on data, substantiated by data, and driven by data. Thus, it is a very natural and innate characteristic of humans to be data-driven!

I am not sure who first said "Knowledge is power", but the phrase has been found in Latin text attributed to the seventeenth-century founder of the modern scientific method, Sir Francis Bacon. There is also some evidence of that phrase in Arabic a full millennium earlier, from the seventh century. It is interesting that Bacon (Sir "Scientific Method" himself) is connected to this very important understanding that knowledge (as derived from data, evidence, and information in conjunction with hypothesis-driven questioning and validation) carries such enormous weight in human affairs. Whether one is fighting the war against cancer, or the battle to stop infectious diseases, or the cybersecurity war, or the battle to win the hearts of your customers, or pricing wars within competitive marketplaces, or engaged in other battles, the winners will most certainly be those who are the most data-driven and have the most knowledge of their domain - those who truly appreciate that knowledge is power.

The era of big data has changed the business and organization landscape radically. We are now on the verge of quantifying and tracking just about everything in our domains – including mobile, social, web, and other digital signals, plus ubiquitous sensors in the Internet of Things (IOT). The technologies that enable and empower this transformation are often referred to as SMAC: social, mobile, analytics, and cloud. All of these technological areas have contributed to and have benefited from data, data, data! In "social" the application of sentiment analysis on social media data is commonplace in many industries. In "mobile" the whole experience is associated with, driven by, and a producer of data! In "analytics," well, you know... it is all about the data – remember that the two most important things in data science are the data and the science (reference: Sir Francis Bacon). And finally, "cloud" computing was developed as a means to share resources (computing and data) easily and on-demand, from anywhere. SMAC technologies are data-driven!

The phrase "360 view" is common jargon in the data analytics conversations of many organizations. Instead of relying on stale, sparse samples and limited demographic attributes, we are now able to explore and exploit fast, wide, and deep data collections about the objects that we care most about. These data can (and will be) augmented by great sources of contextual information (from the IOT) that will truly drive a cognitive analytics revolution in coming years. Our digital sensors (including web logs, social media, mobile interactions, measurement devices, and more) will capture data faster, across a broader set of dimensions, for comprehensively deep samples of the objects in our areas of focus. Consequently, to be a modern digital business is to be data-driven. To be otherwise is to be left behind.

Data drives results for at least three major functional

requirements in any domain (whether it is business, or science, or government, or education, or whatever): discovery, decision-making, and value-creation (i.e., innovation). The best ROI metric (if you can quantify it) would be Return on Innovation through data-driven processes, people, and products.

Data collections are now recognized as a core business asset, a new natural resource, a driver of business change and innovation, a source of increased and/or new revenue streams, a creative force for new products and new markets, and a job opportunity bonanza for those with essential data skills.

One might say that data is the new oil, and there is a pot of gold waiting at the end of the data analytics rainbow within your organization. If you play along with these metaphors for just a moment, you might notice that the way to the golden pinnacle of success is a slippery (oily) slope that is fraught with numerous technological, cultural, and human resource challenges. This shouldn't scare us away from being data-driven. On the contrary, we should embrace this process of discovery and improvement. Someone once said: "Good judgment comes from experience. And experience comes from bad judgment." So, data-driven leadership accepts this process of informed growth and quality improvement.

To address the challenges and rewards that are now facing data-driven leaders, Jay Zaidi has brought us a timely book that is based upon his many years of data management, governance, and analytics experience. This book is not another hype-driven cheerleading treatment of the subject, but it is a practical, evidence-based, and experience-backed look at both the power and the pitfalls of the modern data-driven leader. The key theme is expressed in the book's title – that the way to win the battles that your organization is facing is through the power of data (and knowledge).

To be data-driven is first and foremost the drive to be objective and evidence-based in your organizational decisions. Those decisions involve products (manufacturing, supply chain, placement, pricing, and social/mobile/web content), processes (monitoring, detection, discovery, prediction, and optimization), and people (employees, customers, stakeholders, and new engagement opportunities). This book examines the complexity of this organizational ecosystem in the context of how data informs better outcomes, drives change, and creates new value.

One of the most practical and immediate steps to data-driven success is to recognize the importance and necessity of a new officer in the corporate executive suite. That data-driven officer may have different titles (and roles) in different organizations, but their importance is real: the CDO (chief data officer), the CDS (chief data scientist), or the CAO (chief analytics officer). In some cases, for more market-focused organizations, the chief marketing officer may be the data-driven leader of digital business transformation. This book looks at these roles and reviews the parameters of their duties, the politics that may arise, the perils of the position, and its power to bring winning solutions based upon evidence, facts, and data.

Data-driven discovery, decision-making, and innovation – these are what humans are good at. Shouldn't your leaders be good at them also?

Kirk Borne

Principal Data Scientist
Booz Allen Hamilton
Washington, D.C., U.S.A.
June 2016

PREFACE

Since we live a significant portion of our lives in the digital world, leaving an ever-increasing digital trail, data is being created all the time. Most organizations are seeing their data volumes rise by 30 to 50 percent every year. Private and public sector companies have to manage, govern, and analyze this data to generate insights, manage risk, and create business value. Business leaders have to drive this transformation and culture change by becoming data-driven. This is a complex undertaking, and most organizations and their leaders are struggling to cope. Nimble rivals, much more sophisticated in technology, data management, and data science, are either disrupting traditional competitors or threatening to take over a significant portion of their market share.

In this new world order, organizations must continuously innovate and improvise using data to stay relevant, and leaders must be at the forefront of this transformation. Along with the massive opportunities this data deluge presents, it poses some serious challenges as well. Organizations have to secure sensitive data to ensure its privacy; create golden copies of customer, product, and vendor data (i.e., master data); extract contextual data related to processes and specific data elements; ensure that the quality of business-critical data is constantly monitored and remediated; and confirm that the right level of data governance is in place. This is even more of a business imperative for highly regulated industries, such as those involving financial services, health care, energy and utilities, life sciences, and pharmaceuticals.

Here's some information about me. I founded AlyData, a boutique data management and analytics advisory firm, in 2014. Prior to founding AlyData, I was at Fannie Mae, the largest financial services company in the world, for thirteen years. At Fannie Mae, I directly reported to the chief data officer and led data quality, data governance, data warehouse, master data management, metadata, analytics, and business intelligence programs. I spent seven years in management consulting at PricewaterhouseCoopers LLC and other firms prior to that.

Many books are available on individual topics related to data management, such as data governance, data quality, master data management, business intelligence, and data science. I wanted to write a book that provides a big-picture view of these topics and connects the dots across them, using real-life experiences. My primary goal is to raise awareness and educate readers about the opportunities and challenges related to the emerging fields of strategic data management (SDM) and data science using real world examples and lessons learned, and why a data culture is critical for success. *Being data-savvy and data-driven are core skills for leaders in the "Age of Data".*

This book is intended for the following audiences:

- Senior management, executives, and aspiring leaders at private and public sector companies, since they typically sponsor data-intensive projects and are key decision-makers

- Policymakers in the private and public sectors who are trying to understand the challenges and opportunities that big data and the Internet of Things (IOT) present

- Line managers responsible for planning and executing data-intensive projects

- Data and system analysts and developers looking to expand their knowledge of data management

- Students exploring careers in data management and data science

- Anyone who is curious about the world of enterprise data

With the advent of big data and IOT, companies have to bridge the traditional small data systems with big data to extract maximum value. In addition, they have to expand their quality, governance, and analytics programs to encompass the big data lake(s). My observation is that many companies are still not at the right level of data management maturity on their small data, and that introducing big data into the equation is causing major challenges for their staff and leadership.

Data-Driven Leaders Always Win starts off by describing the "Dawn of Data," in which organizations are being inundated and overwhelmed by data. The next part focuses on the dark side of big data and data quality, followed by an exploration of the perils of not investing in strategic data management. We then dive into the politics of data and who leads, or should lead, the important data function. Next, we delve into the challenges faced by data consumers and the dysfunctional relationship between IT and business organizations and its impact on the organization.

Once we've described the challenges and opportunities related to data management, we discuss the side effects of investing in data management and analytics. Once organizations reach a high level of maturity in data management and analytics and become data-driven, they have an opportunity to monetize data and diversify revenue streams.

The next three parts take a deep dive into the knowledge areas and environmental factors for data management, followed by a discussion of each knowledge area.

The next two sections describe the Data Management Maturity Model, which can be used to develop a roadmap for success, and discuss how senior leaders can make a case for culture change and become data-driven.

The appendix contains a recap of the major themes discussed in the book, a list of data visualization tools, some notes, an index, and a glossary of commonly used data management terms.

By sharing observations, insights, and experiences, and connecting some dots in the process, my hope is that you will gain information that will help you realize the true value of data, become a data evangelist in your organization, and influence your peers and senior management to strategically invest in data management and data science, with the goal of becoming a data-driven organization.

Use the information provided in this book and the questions raised, to trigger a debate within your organization on what your level of data management and data science maturity is and what steps you must take to implement a data culture.

I will close with a quote from Mahatma Gandhi: *"You must be the change you wish to see in the world."*

Go forth and conquer!

Note: I will donate a portion of the proceeds to the India Health Foundation (www.indiahealthfoundation.org), which provides free and highly subsidized healthcare to the poor in India.

ACKNOWLEDGMENTS

Any project of this size isn't possible without the support and encouragement of others. I would like to acknowledge the following people:

- My parents, who made tremendous sacrifices to send me to the best schools, always pushed me to set lofty goals, and then challenged me to achieve them. My father was in the Indian army all his life and retired as a major general. He inculcated in me a sense of discipline and hard work, which has helped me in my academic and professional lives. I am especially grateful to my dear mother, who passed away on February 17, 2015 after courageously battling cancer. She challenged me to be the best that I could be and to never give up. She will always be my inspiration and my role model.

- My dear wife Shabnam, who has stuck with me during thick and thin for the past twenty-two years. I have tested her patience by working on my laptop for hours on end, completing projects or conducting research. She has made tremendous sacrifices, and she never complains (I'm exaggerating a bit). For that I am truly grateful, and I can probably never repay her. I consider this book a joint effort between Shabnam and me, since I couldn't have done this without her support, constructive criticism, and patience.

- My children Ali, Mariam, and Reza, who bring joy and keep me grounded. They are great kids, and I hope and pray that they will become productive citizens and make a positive contribution to this world in their own special ways.

- I would be remiss if I didn't thank the reviewers: Ed Watson (Former EVP and Head of Operations and Technology, Fannie Mae); George Vega (Managing Director, UBS); Beth Hiatt (COO, Unissant and Former CDO, Fannie Mae); Douglas Laney (VP and Distinguished Analyst, Gartner); Kathy Keller (Managing Director, Newbold Advisors); Dr. Raza Hashim (IBM); Samra Sulaiman (Founder, ConsultData LLC); Greg Steffine (Best-selling author and Business Intelligence expert); Patrick Kore (Senior Manager, Peak AML Advisory); and Atul Rao (Manager, Data & Analytics, PricewaterhouseCoopers LLC). They spent many hours reviewing drafts and providing feedback on the content, and helped make this a much better book.

- I should also take this opportunity to thank Dr. Kirk Borne profusely. Upon my insistence, he agreed to write the foreword, despite his extremely hectic consulting, writing, and speaking schedule. Dr. Borne is someone that I admire and respect and am honored that he took time out of his busy schedule to do this for me.

- Finally, I'd like to thank all my teachers and classmates from Hyderabad Public School and Osmania University in India, Texas A&M and Johns Hopkins Universities in the United States, and friends, mentors, coworkers, and extended family that have been there for me during good times and the not so good times. I appreciate their support, encouragement, and prayers.

PART ONE

Dealing With the Data Deluge

Chapter 1

Welcome To the Dawn of Data

I coined the term "The Dawn of Data" to highlight the fact that we are witnessing the emergence of data as a value creator for organizations, which is presenting tremendous growth opportunities for current data practitioners and those aspiring to become data analysts, data engineers, and data scientists. In addition, we will discuss some challenges that must be overcome to derive business value from data.

Numerous data-driven companies have emerged in the last two decades, and have left their traditional rivals in the dust, in terms of societal impact, revenue growth, and constant innovation. Google (Market Cap: $428 billion), Amazon ($250 billion), Facebook ($263 billion), PayPal ($50 billion), eBay ($34 billion), Apple ($690 billion), LinkedIn ($25 billion), Twitter ($30 billion), comScore ($2.35 billion), and Netflix ($48 Billion), for instance, have a combined market capitalization in the trillions of dollars.

Uber and Airbnb are other examples of nimble, data-driven companies that are taking the world by storm and disrupting traditional, well-entrenched rivals. These companies don't own real estate, vehicles, or massive infrastructure. Their business models are based on a sharing economy, and they are targeted at millennials—a very different type of consumer.

"They are data-driven—data is their primary focus and is at the heart of everything they do and they have a proven track record of monetizing data, using data to innovate and to gain a competitive advantage."

Organizations that want to thrive and not get disrupted should emulate these firms - they should pivot around data, use analytics to their advantage, use data-driven insights to innovate, and deliver customer value, with a sense of urgency.

Larry Downes and Paul Nunes explain in their stimulating book, *Big Bang Disruption: Strategy in the Age of Devastating Innovation,* that big-bang disruption is large-scale, fast-paced innovation, which can disrupt stable businesses very rapidly.

"As the computing revolution continues to insinuate itself into every corner of our lives, Big Bang Disrupters are starting to appear in every industry. Outside of computing, exponential growth is also visible... in stem cell research, renewable energy, human genomics fiber optics, LEDs, and robotics. In material science alone, impressive breakthroughs in water splitting, super-capacitors, photonics, thermo-electrics, and energy storage materials... each with the potential for exponential growth..."

Downes and Nunes state that the disruptions are not affecting merely obscure corners of the economy: "Drive down any downtown street and look at the empty storefronts. Many of them were occupied by bookstores, camera retailers and film processors, office supply shops, post offices, travel agencies and big box electronics and appliance sellers."

Blockbuster, Barnes & Noble, Radio Shack, Office Depot, Circuit City, Borders, Staples, Macy's, K-Mart, and J. C. Penney all are examples of brick-and-mortar stores that either shut down or were severely disrupted by nimbler data-driven rivals.

Let me share some facts with you, to set the stage:

- Most organizations are seeing their data volumes rise by 30 to 50 percent every year[1]

- 70 percent of the digital universe is generated by users, but enterprises have responsibility for the storage, security, and management of 80 percent of this data[2]

- There are approximately 1.4 billion mobile phones[3] in the world today, and literally every person is expected to have one within a decade or two

- By 2020[4]

    - Data production will be forty-four times greater than it was in 2009

    - The International Data Corporation (IDC) projects data volume to be 40 zettabytes (40 ZB is 40 billion terabytes or 40 trillion gigabytes)

    - One-third of all data will live in or pass through the cloud

    - IDC estimates that business transactions on the Internet—business-to-business and business-to-consumer—will reach 450 billion per day

We are entering the "Dawn of Data," and organizations are being forced to transition from an information technology–centric world to a data-centric world. ***Information technology will continue to play a critical role, but data must take center stage going forward.***

In this new world reality, organizations must pivot around data and invest in strategic data management, analytics, and data security if they wish to gain a competitive advantage and accomplish their corporate mission.

Since organizations have historically focused on IT, this requires a major shift in focus, starting at the top. It has serious ramifications for the organizational structure and alignment, funding, leadership, talent acquisition and development, business model, strategy, and execution. Due to the strategic nature of the decision to embrace a data-driven culture, these adjust-ments and the associated change management program have to be made at the senior management and board levels.

OPPORTUNITIES

This new reality presents a massive opportunity for organi-zations. Rich online behavior and transaction data acquired from various channels can be integrated to gain deep insights in order to drive marketing and sales, innovation, research and development, product development, mass customization, and advertising.

The tangible observations and opportunities that this cre-ates are:

1. *Cost Savings:* If US healthcare were to use big data cre-atively and effectively to drive efficiency and quality, the sector could create more than $300 billion in value every year. Two-thirds of that would be in the form of reducing US healthcare expenditures by about 8 percent (McKinsey Report on big data[5]). Another example of cost savings is in the developed economies of Europe. Government admin-istrators could save more than €100 billion ($149 billion) in operational efficiency improvements alone by using big data, not including using big data to reduce fraud and er-rors and boost the collection of tax revenues (McKinsey report on big data).

2. *Revenue Generation:* Digi-Capital[6] predicts that revenue from the mobile Internet will top $700 billion annually by 2017, more than tripling its 2014 figure. The vast majority of that, $500 billion, will come from m-commerce, or purchas-es made by people using their phones to order things online.

3. *Faster and Better Insights:* By integrating structured and un-structured data from internal and external sources, organi-zations can gather deep insights in an agile and cost-effective

manner. This applies to every business vertical. A good example is the fact that the genome of a person can now be processed for $1,000.[7]

4. *Innovation:* Big data allows ever-narrower segmentation of customers and, therefore, much more innovative, precisely tailored products or services.

Research indicates that data-driven organizations are more successful than their peers. Median return on investment (ROI) for top performing organizations that use data predictive analytics is 145 percent, compared to 89 percent for those that don't, and they see a 6 percent increase in annual customer retention compared to a 1 percent decrease for the others.

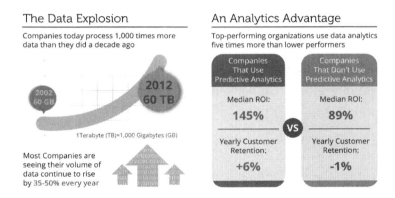

Figure 1.1 Power in Data *(Source: IBM)*

CHALLENGES

The significant increase in the volume of unstructured data (e.g., photos, videos, and social media) has ushered in a new breed of NoSQL and big data technologies. These new tools and technologies enable the processing of large amounts of multi-format data in a cost-effective manner, but they are evolving in terms of maturity. This presents architectural and operational challenges.

There are five primary challenges that the data tsunami creates for organizations:

1. *Data Management and Security:* Decentralized storage and democratization of data complicates the data governance, information security, and data quality dimensions.

2. *Costs:* Costs related to the storage and management of data will grow significantly unless organizations take proactive measures to address this.

3. *Complexity:* Organizations face a dual challenge—they must manage and support traditional structured data stores while building out NoSQL and Hadoop stores in order to process and analyze massive amounts of unstructured data to address business needs.

4. *Skills:* Given the dynamic nature of this environment and the speed at which innovation is occurring, finding the right talent will be difficult. Organizations can retrain business, IT, and operations staff in data management, data security, and analytics to address this issue.

5. *Data Foundation:* Despite all the hype, current research indicates that less than half of all employees find that corporate information helps them get their jobs done. The problem of getting the right information to the right people at the right time is getting worse, given the growing number of information sources, uses, and users.

In order to appreciate the value data brings to organizations, leaders and associates have to gain a high level of data literacy and sophistication about the fields of data management and data science.

The Data Journalism Handbook[8] provides a good definition of data literacy - *"Data literacy is the ability to consume for knowledge, produce coherently and think critically about data. Data literacy includes statistical literacy, but also insights into how to work with large data sets, how they were produced, how to connect various data sets and how to interpret them."*

There are many aspects of data management (e.g., governance, quality, metadata, and master and reference data), data security, and analytics that have to be considered and prioritized for organizations to become data-driven. Each organization operates at a different level of maturity with respect to IT, data management, and enterprise architecture and has to address capability gaps accordingly. *Pivoting around data and considering new strategies and investments from that lens will serve it well.*

If they haven't already, organizations must develop a strategic data management plan, a strategy for data security and analytics, and a data management roadmap and implementation plan that align with the business and IT strategy to address capability gaps.

Embark, with a sense of urgency, on a journey to become truly data-driven and reap the benefits. If the scope of this effort is daunting, you may consider implementing it opportunistically, at the department level first, and expand it to the enterprise in stages.

Welcome to the "Dawn of Data!" Jump on the data bandwagon—to learn, grow, and flourish, and to make sure your organization doesn't get disrupted by a nimbler data-driven rival.

Five Takeaways and Action Items

1. Organizations that want to thrive, and not get disrupted, should emulate data-driven firms such Google, Facebook, and Apple—pivot around data, use analytics to the organization's advantage, use data-driven insights to innovate, and deliver customer value with a sense of urgency.

2. Information technology will continue to play a critical role, but data must take center stage going forward. Organizations that wish to become data-driven will have to transform themselves, including changing their culture, introducing new tools and technologies, upgrading the skills of employees or hiring employees with strong data skills, and looking at ways to monetize data assets.

3. There are many opportunities to monetize, save costs, and innovate using big data.

4. To implement big data, organizations will have to deal with a few challenges, such as technical complexity, skill gaps, data management and security risks, and costs.

5. Organizations should implement big data opportunistically, based on their specific business needs and the competitive landscape.

Chapter 2

Data-Driven Leaders Always Win

I n a short life span of fifty-six years, Steve Jobs revolutionized no fewer than six different industries: *personal computers, mobile phones, music publishing, animated films, digital publishing, and tablet computing.* It's a pretty impressive track record for someone who was adopted at birth, dropped out of college after the first semester, dropped LSD and smoked marijuana, wandered off to India to find himself, became a businessman, got fired from the company he founded, and returned with a vengeance – *like a Phoenix rising from the ashes.* It's quite a story and a pretty impressive one at that.

I've been a Steve Jobs fan for years, followed him and his company, bought numerous Apple products over the years, and absorbed some of his principles into my life. Steve certainly had his negative personality traits and many detractors, but he was human after all. A few things that impressed me the most about him were his passion for innovation, his phenomenal design aesthetics, his laser-like focus on quality, and his disregard for material wealth. Here is a quote from Steve that clearly articulates his thoughts about innovation:

"Innovation has nothing to do with how many R & D dollars you have. When Apple came up with the Mac, IBM was spending at least 100 times more on R & D. It's not about money. It's about the people you have, how you're led, and how much you get it."

This chapter is meant to show business leaders that they have a vested interest in ensuring that data is treated as a strategic asset, that business teams must take accountability for it, and that there should be an ongoing investment in data management and analytics, to innovate and win.

Why specifically focus on business leaders? *It's because business leaders, like chief executive officers (CEOs), CMOs, chief risk officers (CROs), and chief financial officers (CFOs), are on the front lines*—developing business strategies, driving product innovation, and selling products and services, constantly working to gain competitive advantage and driving shareholder value. This is no mean task, and they need every arrow in their quiver—data being one. What they have to realize is that **data is their friend.** They shouldn't shy away from it, but embrace it with open arms, invest in it, take ownership of it, and be accountable for its governance.

We are in the midst of a digital revolution, resulting from the confluence of social, mobile, analytics, and cloud data, and we finally have the tools and technology to process massive amounts of disparate data to gain deep insights. Businesses can now find the unknown unknowns (i.e., The Johari Window[1]) and use the insights gleaned from data to create new products, improve services, get to know their customers better, provide highly personalized offerings to customers, and predict the future with a high degree of certainty.

So, what's holding businesses back? *The primary reason businesses aren't able to achieve their full potential is that business leaders aren't "<u>standing up for data.</u>"* Rather than just *lean in*, they should *stand up* for data.

"Standing up for data" means that business leaders must do the following five things:

1. *Treat data as a strategic asset.* Give it more importance than physical assets such as buildings and infrastructure.

2. *Take ownership for the governance of their data assets,* rather than delegating this important function to the information technology department or some other team.

3. *Invest in the quality of business-critical data.*

4. *Clearly articulate the questions that they want answered,* and challenge their IT and data departments to use all the data assets to answer them.

5. *Always ask these questions when making decisions based on data:*

    ◆ Where did this data come from?

    ◆ Who is accountable for the definition and governance of this data?

    ◆ What's been done to this data (i.e., transformation)?

    ◆ Does this data meet our quality requirements, and what are the data quality metrics associated with it?

Data-driven leaders always win! Let me close with this quote from Steve:

"Being the richest man in the cemetery doesn't matter to me. Going to bed at night saying we've done something wonderful, that's what matters to me."

Four Takeaways and Action Items

1. Business leaders must increase their data IQ and awareness of the field of data management and analytics.

2. Innovation has very little to do with research and development (R&D) dollars; instead it's about the people you have, how you're led, and how much you get it. Leaders play a key role in this.

3. Business leaders must not just "Lean In" but they should "Stand Up" for data.

4. There are 5 tangible things that leaders can do: (1) treat data as a strategic asset, (2) take ownership of governance of their assets, (3) invest to ensure the quality of their critical enterprise data assets, (4) question the veracity, lineage, and accuracy of data, and (5) challenge their IT and data departments to improve the maturity of the data management functions.

Chapter 3

Are You a Data-Driven Leader?

Data-driven organizations require a different type of leader. A transition from Corporate Leadership 1.0 to Corporate Leadership 2.0 is underway—a new leadership model that takes into account the current realities of democratized and decentralized data, an organization's ability to harness its power, and the missing fourth pillar of technology management.

You are probably wondering what the fourth pillar alludes to and what the other three pillars are? Keep reading, and you'll find out.

The impetus for this chapter was a recent conversation I had with the chief operating officer of a healthcare organization. His company had recently acquired a competitor, and it was dealing with the typical post acquisition challenges related to people, process, and technology - the three pillars for managing technology. In addition, he had inherited a host of other operational issues. But a fourth, and most important, pillar wasn't on the COO's radar. The board expected him to streamline the operations of the combined entity and deliver results within two quarters.

Corporate Leadership 1.0. Corporate Leadership 1.0 was the era of people, process, and technology. Those were considered the three legs of *the golden triangle* of managing information technology (IT), and they applied to all industry verticals and to organizations of all sizes. This concept was articulated in the 1960s and has served us well. Most executives know it and use it to strategize, plan, and execute IT projects.

Corporate Leadership 2.0. Fast-forward to 2015. IT is now a mature field and can be considered a streamlined service offering. Cloud computing is fast becoming a must-have service and is providing organizations an opportunity to deliver software and infrastructure quickly. We take e-mail for granted. Networks work and transmit hundreds of terabytes of data seamlessly. Provisioning storage in the cloud is quite straightforward, software deployment is relatively painless, and technical support can be delivered across the globe and around the clock.

Transformation from Corporate Leadership 1.0 to Corporate Leadership 2.0. Given this IT scenario, Corporate Leadership 2.0 requires leaders to focus on data as a strategic asset while continuing to leverage their IT infrastructure. This will enable organizations to derive crucial insights to propel them forward and achieve their mission. In the Leadership 2.0 model, leaders must focus on the fourth pillar of technology management, which is data.

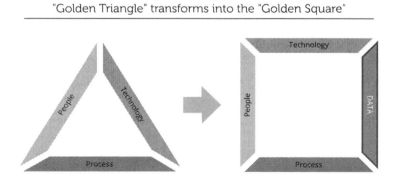

Figure 3.1 "Golden Triangle" Transforms into the "Golden Square"

I've developed a new concept called "the golden square". In the new model, the three-legged "golden triangle" transforms into a four legged "golden square": <u>People, Process, Technology, and Data.</u>

Board Members, visionary leaders, and their organizations should start using the "golden square" terminology and incorporating this new concept into all their programs.

A recent synthesis of a large body of the literature on leading knowledge workers (Amar and Hlupic 2012[1]) reveals that, in order to foster innovation in knowledge-based organizations, a different leadership style is needed, based on horizontal rather than vertical leadership, where power and authority are distributed on the basis of knowledge.

"In this new management model, data will play a critical role in organizations where decisions are made and power and authority are distributed on the basis of knowledge, rather than organizational hierarchy."

Let me bring this back full circle to my conversation with the COO and the reason for this chapter. The first thing the COO asked for was a dashboard that would reveal the health of each of his business units, the risk exposure across them, and opportunities for improvement. He identified key performance indicators related to sales, expenses, profit-and-loss, labor costs, human resources, vendor management, contracts, overheads, budgets, and so forth. He also asked for competitive intelligence and wanted us to benchmark his new organization against its peers and provide recommendations on how he could streamline operations, reduce overhead, increase automation, and improve the bottom line.

You will notice that the common thread across all these "asks" was data. We utilized data discovery, data quality, master data, contextual data, data virtualization, Lean Six Sigma, business intelligence, and analytics (e.g., predictive, prescriptive, and descriptive) to satisfy our client's requests.

"Your main constituencies are your employees, your customers and your products." - Jack Welch, ex-CEO, General Electric

---

Infrastructure, software, and technology were used for this exercise, but the primary value creator was the data. We unleashed its power by generating deep insights across three dimensions—employees, customers, and products. These insights drove tactical and strategic decisions related to the combined organization's employees, customers, and products.

The two important points to take away are: (1) the new leadership model pivots around data, and (2) the three-legged "golden triangle" transforms into a four-legged "golden square"—*People, Process, Technology and Data.*

Data-driven leaders should start focusing on "the golden square" across all programs, so that data is treated as a strategic asset. This new model has ramifications not just on the culture of the organization and skill development, but on the organizational model as well. The leadership team and human resource department will have to address these items.

Six Takeaways and Action Items

1. We are transitioning from Corporate Leadership 1.0 to Corporate Leadership 2.0—a new leadership model that takes into account the current realities of democratized and decentralized data, an organization's ability to harness its power.

2. Corporate Leadership 2.0 requires leaders to focus on data as a strategic asset while continuing to leverage their IT infrastructure. This will enable organizations to derive insights to propel them forward and achieve their mission.

3. We have introduced a new concept called "the golden square." In the new model, the three-legged "golden triangle" transforms into a four-legged "golden square"—people, process, technology, and data. This has ramification on the culture and organization model.

4. Organizations must start focusing on "the golden square"—people, process, technology, and data—across all programs and change the internal dialog. Without a focus on data, they will not be able to scale and stay competitive.

5. Data-driven leaders appreciate the tremendous value that data and analytics bring to their organization, are well versed in the field of data management, and know what questions to ask of their teams with respect to the quality, lineage, systems of truth, and the analysis conducted on data to generate reports and insights.

6. The strategy investments in data management, quality, and governance that data-driven leaders make will not just result in better business outcomes, but can also be a driver for creation of new products and lines of business—by monetizing data

Chapter 4

Data Needs a Seat at the Table

The focus of this chapter is on the five primary reasons why the data management function deserves a seat at the C-level table and needs to get the investment and sponsorship from the chief executive officer and board.

Here they are:

1. The small and big data ecosystems within organizations are very complex.

2. Data is pervasive and used by every department within the organization. Consumers demand high quality and timely access to data.

3. Data management, analytics, and governance are critical to extract business value and mitigate risks.

4. Most companies are seeing their data volumes rise by 30 to 50 percent every year.

5. Data-driven organizations are more successful than their peers.

A few points to bolster our case:

Business Value Proposition

Median ROI[1] for top performing organizations that use data predictive analytics is 145 percent compared to 89 percent for those that don't, and they see a 6 percent increase in annual customer retention compared to a 1 percent decrease for others.

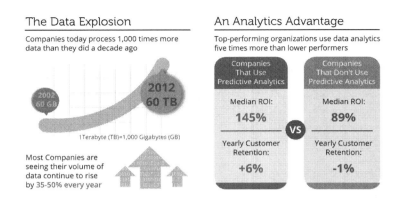

Figure 4.1 Power in Data *(Source: IBM)*

Application Scenarios for Big Data

Every department will benefit from the use of data, from increased sales to optimized logistics.

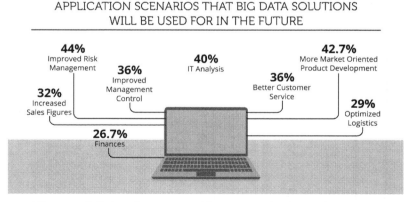

Figure 4.2 Applications That Benefit from Big Data

Big data can be analyzed to deliver deeper customer insights, identify cost savings, detect fraud, better manage risk, and deliver process efficiency.

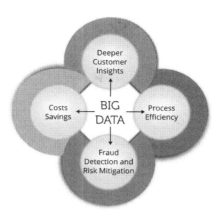

Figure 4.3 Typical Big Data Use Cases

Complex Data Ecosystem

If you aren't familiar with your organization's small data eco-systems, you certainly should be. If you are lucky to find a current copy, I bet it looks something like the highly siloed, fragmented, and complex ecosystem below.

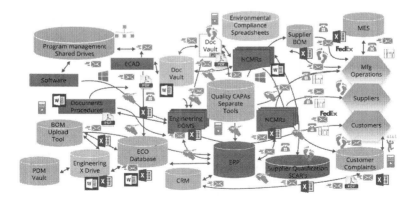

Figure 4.4 Data Silos in Medium to Large Size Organizations
(Source: Stan Przybylinski[2] of CIMData)

Imagine introducing a big data lake into the mix, to create a single store for processing enterprise data. This would further complicate data sourcing, integration, and data wrangling processes. It would also require additional effort and tooling to catalog data as it flows into the lake, in order to capture lineage, secure sensitive data, manage user access (i.e., all aspects of data governance), and ensure the quality of data across the small and big data worlds.

The diagram below shows a highly structured and simplified view of a Unified Data Architecture[3] (UDA). This architecture supports the ingestion and processing of real-time streaming data as well as that of unstructured data in batch mode.

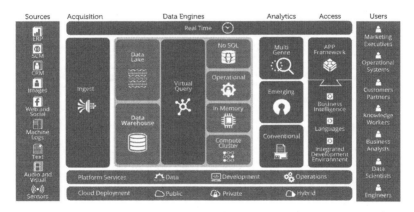

Figure 4.5 Unified Data Architecture *(Source: Teradata[3])*

The UDA has a provision for maintaining the existing data warehouse(s) as the data lake is introduced into the ecosystem.

The small and big data ecosystem is going to reside in a hybrid cloud environment (i.e., public and private cloud) and has to be integrated into numerous cloud-based services.

The diagram below visualizes how the twenty-first century cloud spaghetti[4] architecture that looms large.

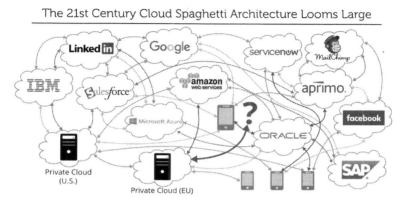

Figure 4.6 Twenty-First Century Cloud Spaghetti Architecture Looms Large *(Source: Gartner)*

Data Explosion

Data is exploding across all sectors. Discrete manufacturing, government, telecommunications and media, process manufacturing, banking, and healthcare are the top six of these sectors.

Big Data

As the amount of data used by businesses grows, there are new opportunities for analyzing it, which stands to change how we make day-to-day business decisions. One Petabyte is equivalent to 1 million gigabytes. A large ipod has a capacity of 160 gigabytes.

Sector	Data Stored in the U.S., in Petabytes (2009)	Petabytes Per Firm*
	0 200 400 600 800 1000	
Discrete Manufacturing		0.94
Government		1.28
Communications/Media		1.75
Process Manufacturing		0.81
Banking		1.89
Health- Care Providers		0.36
Securities/Investment Services		3.78
Professional Services		0.27
Retail		0.68

*For firms with more than 1,000 employees   Source: McKinsey Global Institute analysis of data from IDC (data stored) and U.S.Dept of Labor

Figure 4.7 New Opportunities for Analyzing Big Data[5] *(Source: McKinsey Global Institute)*

Sensor technology (IOT) and smartphones, as well as social media applications, are responsible for the rapid rise in data volumes.

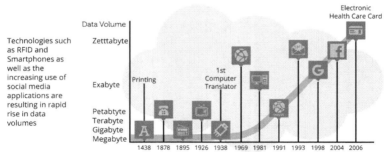

Exponential Growth of Data Volumes

Source: Federal Association of Information Technology, Telecommunication and New Media |BITKOM|.

Figure 4.8 Exponential Growth of Data Volumes *(Source: BITKOM)*

Drivers for Information Overload

There are three primary drivers for the data explosion—online, mobile, and social.

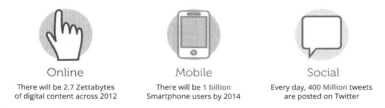

Online
There will be 2.7 Zettabytes
of digital content across 2012

Mobile
There will be 1 billion
Smartphone users by 2014

Social
Every day, 400 Million tweets
are posted on Twitter

Figure 4.9 Power in Data *(Source: IBM)*

External Data Can Augment Internal Data

Organizations typically focus on internal data to generate insights. They shouldn't lose sight of the rich external data such as social media data, audio, photos and video that are available from various channels to enrich internal data – to deliver better insights.

Five Takeaways and Action Items

1. Data is exploding across all sectors. Discrete manufacturing, government, telecommunications and media, process manufacturing, banking, and healthcare are the top six.

2. Data management deserves a seat at the highest rungs of the organization because it is the lifeblood of the business, it is used in deriving insights that are critical for operating businesses, it is growing at a rate of 30 to 50 percent per year, and data-driven organizations are more successful than their peers are.

3. Big data has application in risk management, product development, customer service, IT analysis, increased sales, finances, and improvement management controls.

4. Sensor technology (IOT) and smartphones, as well as social media applications, are responsible for the rapid rise in data volumes.

5. There are three primary drivers for the data explosion—online, mobile, and social.

PART TWO

Unleash Dark Data and Understand the Dark Side of Data

Chapter 5

Got Dark Data? Find and Unleash It

Organizations are swimming in data; in fact, they are drowning in data. A significant portion of this data is collected, processed, and stored, but never utilized for any meaningful purpose—it goes into a black hole. Gartner calls this "Dark Data". John Kelly, IBM's "father of Watson" said the following at an IBM Cognitive Computing event held in San Francisco in October 2015[1]: "80% of all data is dark and unstructured. We can't read it or use it in our computing systems. By 2020, that number will be 93%." At the same time, we are generating a million GB of health data for each person during a lifetime, and there are 7 billion people on the earth. By 2020, cars will be generating 350MB of data per second "and that data will need to be assessed", he noted.

Dark Data is a major liability from a privacy and security perspective, consumes a significant portion of the CIO's infrastructure and operating budget, and there is an opportunity cost associated with it.

So, why aren't organizations looking at this from a liability and opportunity perspective? There are three primary reasons:

1. They have a limited view into their data inventory, since they operate in silos.

2. They have limited or no data discovery capability.

3. Their data governance programs aren't mature enough.

Chief finance officers and chief information security officers (CISOs) are on point to address the expense and risk sides of this equation and the chief marketing officer is tasked with addressing it from an opportunity perspective. They have to decide whether their organizations will convert Dark Data from a liability into an asset, stop acquiring more of it, or jettison it.

To put things in perspective, the data tsunami is here and the situation is going to get worse. Organizations should start taking proactive measures to convert their Dark Data into an asset by developing a data inventory, implementing sophisticated data discovery capabilities, and investing in a data governance program.

Once they are able to find and integrate all their data, they will be able to use analytic capabilities to derive business intelligence and insights.

There are various tools available in the marketplace to address these capabilities. The first step is for senior executives to acknowledge that there is a Dark Data problem within their organizations, and the rest will follow.

Five Takeaways and Action Items

1. A significant portion of this data is collected, processed, and stored but never utilized for any meaningful purpose—it goes into a black hole. This is called Dark Data, and IDC estimates put it at 80 percent of the total data acquired.

2. Dark Data is a major liability from a privacy and security perspective, it consumes a significant portion of the CIO's infrastructure and operating budget, and there is an opportunity cost associated with it.

3. The data tsunami is here, and the situation is going to get worse. Organizations should start taking proactive measures to convert their Dark Data into an asset by developing a data inventory, implementing sophisticated data discovery capabilities, and investing in a data governance program.

4. There are various tools available in the marketplace to address these capabilities.

5. The first step is for senior executives to acknowledge that there is a Dark Data problem.

Chapter 6

To Compete, Leaders Must
Liberate 85 percent Of Their Data

n the chapter titled "Got Dark Data? Find and Unleash It," I address the fact that organizations are drowning in data, but that 80 percent of this data (also known as Dark Data) is collected, processed, and stored but never utilized for any meaningful purpose—it goes into the proverbial black hole. Adding to this, another 5 percent or more is *locked up in silos* and protected by data owners, preventing others from using it. I call these "data fiefdoms."

To put things in perspective for you, let me share a statistic published by IDC in April 2014[1]: "From 2013 to 2020, the digital universe will grow by a factor of 10—from 4.4 trillion gigabytes to 44 trillion. It more than doubles every two years."

Dark Data and data fiefdoms account for at least 85 percent of data across all organizations. We're talking about five to ten trillion gigabytes of data, at a minimum. Please take a moment to let the enormity and the implication of this information sink in.

"Opportunity is knocking!
Will organizations answer the door? Will you?"

The inability of an organization to use 85 percent of the data it possesses, for any meaningful purpose, has serious consequences and a devastating impact to its bottom line and mission.

Here are a few consequences:

Cost: Operational and capital expenses related to the collection, processing, and storage of 85 percent of the data are massive. In most instances, all of this data is backed up, archived for several years, and replicated across silos. Hence, the costs grow exponentially year after year.

Opportunity Cost: Opportunity cost, due to the inability to access and utilize the data in a timely manner, is a problem.

Erosion of the Bottom Line: Lack of meaningful use of 85 percent of the data impacts an organization's ability to innovate, drive better insights, and gain competitive advantage—directly eroding its bottom line.

Impact to the Mission: The cost, opportunity cost, and erosion of the bottom line impacts an organization's mission.

Risk Exposure: Processing and storing large amounts of personal and financial data significantly increases risk from theft and cybercrime. There is massive fallout if this data is compromised.

Morale: The morale of the staff suffers when staffers are unable to access and utilize data that is critical to their success.

Waste: There is a significant wastage of human resources, processing power, and time as a result of collecting, processing, and storing 85 percent of an organization's data. These resources could be diverted to value-added activities to directly increase shareholder value and bottom-line results.

Environmental Impact: The servers and storage devices used in the collection, processing, and storage of massive amounts of data consume electricity and cooling capacity and emit heat—resulting in a significant environmental impact.

Please do a back-of-the-envelope calculation and determine the impact of Dark Data and data fiefdoms on your organization's bottom line and its mission. It will change your attitude toward data utilization and get your senior management's attention as well. It's high time we put the "fish on the table"!

Four Takeaways and Action Items

1. 85 percent of an organization's data is locked up in silos and protected by Data Owners who prevent others from using it. I call these data fiefdoms. We're talking about five to ten trillion gigabytes of data, at a minimum.

2. Data more than doubles every two years.

3. The consequences of not dealing with Dark Data results in opportunity cost, higher expenses, an impact to mission goals, waste, morale issues, and risk exposure.

4. Dark Data and data fiefdoms directly impact an organization's bottom line and its mission.

Chapter 7

Bad Data Is Costing the United States at Least 6 percent of its GDP

Bad data has a significant negative impact on an organization's operations and its bottom line. However, surveys indicate that there is a lack of awareness among leaders and their associates about this. It is important for them to be aware of its root causes and to quantify the associated cost so that proactive steps can be taken to improve the quality of data.

The field of cybersecurity and hackers get lots of press and, therefore, making a strong case for investing in cybersecurity is easy and straightforward. Budgets for information security are growing, since senior leaders feel an immediate impact from customers and internal stakeholders when their organization's data is compromised. Loss of personal and financial data is tangible. For organizations, the result is reputation loss, financial loss, and a loss of credibility with customers, and the damage can last for years.

The Target Corporation hack[1] is a great example. The data breach and subsequent compromise of forty million debit and credit card numbers, as well as personal information for another seventy million people, resulted in the firing of the CEO and CIO and a significant drop in revenue. Target had to strengthen its data security and data governance processes, compensate the victims, and introduce new and improved credit cards to mitigate future risks. Its stock price was impacted, and it will take many years for it to recover the customers' trust.

The cost and impact of data quality on an organization's bottom line is the same, or could even be greater, than that of cybercrimes, but they seldom gain as much publicity. No C-level executives have been fired as a result of producing or consuming bad data. This is primarily due to a lack of awareness about the impact of bad data among leadership teams. The impact and cost of bad data on an organization's bottom line are hard to quantify, organizations aren't measuring them, and they are bundled into the operational costs of individual departments.

Let me reiterate a very important point—data quality is a nebulous term, and is hard to quantify; since data is pervasive, most companies do not have a mechanism to quantify data quality across their information supply chains (ISC) and, hence, are unable to determine the impact of bad data on their bottom line. However, most business and operations staff can provide anecdotal evidence and specific examples regarding the impact of bad data on their organization's bottom line.

In 2002, The Data Warehousing Institute (TDWI) published a report titled "Data Quality and the Bottom Line: Achieving Business Success through a Commitment to High Quality Data."[2] This report showed that there is a significant gap between perception and reality regarding the quality of data in many organizations, and that data quality problems cost US businesses more than $600 billion a year. The report's findings were based on interviews with industry experts, leading-edge customers, and survey data from 647 respondents, and it primarily focused on the impacts of bad customer and address data. Imagine what the current costs are, fourteen years later, considering data volumes have exploded due to social and mobile applications and data is far more complex with respect to variety.

Conservative projections put the current impact of bad data and data quality issues on US businesses at $1 trillion dollars. To put this in perspective, the US gross domestic product (GDP) is approximately $17 trillion dollars. ***At a minimum, bad data is costing the United States 6 percent of its GDP. The global impact may be in the trillions of dollars.*** These staggering numbers should get the attention of policymakers, shareholders, and boards of directors!

In a blog post regarding the cost of data quality[3], Jim Harris states: "It always seems crazy to me that few executives base their 'corporate wagers' on the statistical research touted by data quality authors such as Tom Redman, Jack Olson, and Larry English that shows that 15 to 45 percent of the operating expense of virtually all organizations is **WASTED** due to data quality issues."

I read a very well-written article[4] titled "The Causes, Cost and Consequences of Bad Government Data," authored by Katherine Barrett and Richard Green, in which the authors focus on the impact of bad government data in great detail. They identify several root causes for bad data - old systems that make it very difficult to analyze and extract data, minimal sharing of data between technology systems (i.e., siloed systems), bad data definitions compromising the meaning of the information collected, data issues created by third-party contractors, ineffective controls (e.g., common use of Excel spreadsheets), undertrained workers, and the fact that too much access to data increases vulnerability.

The good news is that a significant portion of the wasted operating expenses can be avoided, given a relatively small investment in data quality best practices, tooling, and some awareness building and training.

Here are the seven root causes that we have identified for the high cost of bad data:

1. Data Processing

   - Inefficient processing and project delays, resulting from poor data quality, impacts time-to-value.

   - Data quality checks and data cleansing performed by each data consumer within individual departments is expensive and resource intensive.

   - Organizations that aren't mature from a data quality perspective typically identify and address data quality issues manually. This is error prone, time consuming, and expensive. Lack of automation and repeatable processes impacts the bottom line.

- Redundant data reconciliation checks and remediation is performed across departments, since they operate in silos.

- Root-cause analysis and due diligence performed to address data quality issues is expensive.

2. Decision-Making

- Analytics performed on bad data result in bad outcomes with serious consequences.

3. Financial

- Redundant data quality checks that occur across data silos while being transported across the information supply chain (ETL Processing) is expensive and error prone.

4. Reputation and Brand Impact

- Bad customer data impacts reputation, frustrates customers, impacts decision-making, and leads to a lack of 360-degree views of customers. This is true of other data domains such as product.

5. Regulatory Compliance

- Bad data complicates and makes compliance activities and processes expensive. Therefore, companies are forced to invest in proactive data quality management.

6. Risk Exposure

- Risk management is based on data and facts. Using bad or low quality data to make risk management decisions is not desirable and can have serious ramifications for organizations.

7. Development Costs

    • The development costs incurred by organizations, to work around all their bad data, are significant.

Bad data has a tangible impact on organizations and the productivity of their employees. Data-driven leaders must take measures to tackle the bad data problems by implementing data quality–related policies and standards and investing in awareness building and training and data quality tools. The quality of data must be measured and remediated at the source (i.e., channels and data stores that acquire data) before it is distributed for consumption downstream.

Five Takeaways and Action Items

1. The field of cybersecurity and hackers get lots of press and, therefore, making a strong case for investing in cybersecurity is easy and straightforward.

2. CISO budgets continue to grow even though the losses from cybercrimes are less than those from data quality issues.

3. At a minimum, bad data is costing the United States 6 percent of its GDP. The worldwide impact may be in the trillions.

4. The good news is that a significant portion of the wasted operating expenses can be avoided with a relatively small investment in data quality best practices, tooling, and some training.

5. There are seven primary reasons for the cost of bad data. These are (1) data processing, (2) decision-making, (3) financial, (4) reputation, (5) compliance, (6) risk exposure, and (7) development costs.

Chapter 8

Data Quality Is Job 1 and Here's Why

"Quality is Job 1."
—*Ford Motor Company Slogan*

It was fascinating when the Ford Motor Company introduced this slogan in the 1980s.[1] An American automotive icon was going to use this message to show its customers and employees that it truly cared about the quality of its products and that it would focus on quality at every stage, from product concept to final assembly.

The message resonated with customers and employees and probably had something to do with the fact that Ford Motors was the only American automotive company that didn't ask for a government handout when the financial markets collapsed in 2008.[2]

Jacques Nasser was Ford's CEO in the 80's. His vision was to make Ford a leading consumer products company. In order to achieve this vision, Ford had to focus intensely on customers and make customer satisfaction its highest priority. To win over customers Ford didn't just decide to overhaul its quality processes; it redefined the way it approached its business. Instead of acting like the manufacturing behemoth that it was, Ford wanted to be known as a consumer products company producing high quality products. The quality initiatives[3] instituted saved Ford $300 million in reduced scrap, rework, and nonvalue-added activities. This is equivalent to $754 million in today's dollars[4] – a significant savings.

Slogans such as "Data is the new oil," "Data is the new electricity," or "Data is an organization's lifeblood" are commonly used—but most organizations do not truly appreciate what they mean. Data courses through the veins of every organization but is usually taken for granted, until something goes wrong: there are financial disclosure issues, accounts don't reconcile, the regulator raises alarms, or the internal audit department flags items for review. I address this topic in light of big data and IOT in the chapter titled *The Dark Side of Big Data.*

You are probably wondering what the slogan of an automotive company has to do with data quality. It has a lot to do with data quality, and here's why:

Decisions: Organizations rely on data to make critical business decisions. Using low quality data results in low quality decisions—not something that is desirable.

Policies: Business leaders develop policies based on data. Basing policies on low quality data results in poor policies that have a detrimental effect on end users and aren't optimal.

Reports, Forecasts, and Projections: Data is the raw material used for financial and operational reporting, forecasting, and projections that feed into strategic planning.

Lessons Learned from Ford's Quality Initiative

Here are some lessons learned from Ford's initiative, which can benefit any organization wanting to implement a quality program:

- A program of this magnitude will have to deal with skeptical employees, resource allocation, and data availability.

- Any major change initiative hinges on two factors— complete buy-in from senior leadership and a dedication to understanding customer needs.

- Top leadership should be trained in the quality concepts, methodology, and implementation details. After this, the training should be rolled out quickly throughout the company.

- To accelerate quality improvement efforts, companies should identify the top twenty-five data consumer concerns and assign data quality improvement projects for them.

- A complete continuous improvement process for quality should be implemented. It can be based on Six Sigma's Define, Measure, Analyze, Improve and Control (DMAIC) cycle.

What I'd like you to do is take a minute to focus on the critical data that is used in your daily activities and determine whether anyone within your organization actually *defines quality requirements for them, assesses their quality regularly, and addresses quality issues proactively!* If the answer is "no" or "maybe," you should start doing something about it immediately. If the answer is "yes," then you are in the minority and deserve a pat on the back and special recognition.

There is one more important point that must be noted. Most companies look at their data stores and business processes as isolated components. What I'd like you to do is to change your mind-set, start looking at your business value chain (BVC) and align the associated data into an information supply chain (ISC). By linking the two together and looking at *the quality of data flowing through it as a supply chain problem,* you will be able to start measuring quality across the ISC, determine its impact on the business processes, and make the required quality adjustments.

Data quality matters, and organizations need to focus on it if they want to make better decisions, develop effective policies, and want to improve their strategic planning processes. Ford Motor Company is a perfect example of an automotive giant that focused on quality to gain competitive advantage and changed its culture, *since quality isn't something that can be mandated, but has to become a part of your organization's DNA!* I propose you talk to your management team about introducing a new slogan: "Data Quality Is Job 1" within your organization.

Seven Takeaways and Action Items

1. The CEO of Ford initiated a campaign focused on quality. The goal was to show its customers and employees that it truly cared about the quality of its products and that it would focus on quality at every stage, from product concept to final assembly.

2. This focus on quality resulted in turning the company around and made Ford the top US automaker.

3. This has direct applicability with the quality of data, since it is used for decision-making, forecasting and projections, risk management, operations, and policymaking.

4. Slogans such as "Data is the new oil," "Data is the new electricity" or "Data is an organization's lifeblood" are commonly used—but most organizations do not truly appreciate what they mean and only pay them lip service.

5. The quality of data is usually taken for granted, until something goes wrong, and there are financial disclosure issues, accounts don't reconcile, the regulator raises alarms, or the internal audit department flags items for review.

6. Organizations must proactively define quality requirements, measure them, and remediate issues as a standard operating procedure.

7. Quality isn't something that can be mandated; it must become a part of your organization's DNA and be incorporated into everything it does.

Chapter 9

The Dark Side of Big Data

n June 2015 I was on a panel discussion titled "The Dark Side of Big Data: What Happens When It Falls into the Wrong Hands and Why Regulators Are So Interested."[1] There were three panelists—Rich Licato, the CISO of the Airline Reporting Corporation, John Steven, the chief technology officer (CTO) of Cigital, and me. The discussion was moderated by Ray Vazquez, the CEO of Infinitive Insight.

The title "The Dark Side of Big Data" was prompted by a conversation Ray had with Anne Neuberger, the CRO of the National Security Agency (NSA) while on a train ride to New York City from Washington D.C.

Here's what Anne said:

"In the wrong hands or without the right safeguards, there is a dark side to big data. I doubt consumers truly understand the breadth of data collected about them each day by the private sector."

Most of us are familiar with the massive data breaches that have occurred and continue to occur regularly, compromising the personal and financial information of millions of people. This is one dimension of the dark side of big data, the democratization and decentralization of data, that is providing greater opportunities for the bad guys to get their hands on sensitive and private data.

Another equally important and often overlooked dimension of the dark side of big data is its quality. Let me share a real world example to make my point. My firm was hired by a large medical practice to help solve a complex case. My client was notified by a government agency that it had committed fraud based on medical claims data analyzed by the agency. The firm was told that its billing data and procedures performed were benchmarked against its peers, and the agency had concluded that the charges were excessive. Criminal and civil penalties were being brought, which would result in significant financial penalties and potential jail time.

Put yourself in the shoes of the physicians who worked at this practice. Their livelihoods, reputations, professional careers, and even their freedom, were all at stake. Imagine what they were going through. Add to this the impact this case had on the care and well-being of the thousands of patients they serve.

My intention is not to judge the merits of the case. The point I'm making is that data, and the results of data analysis, can have a major impact on human beings and businesses if they aren't managed well and lack the right level of quality.

We met with the founder and lead physician at the firm and interviewed him at length to determine the facts for ourselves. It was clear to us that his firm had acted in good faith and had tried to follow all the federal government policies and guidelines. It was also clear that these physicians had optimized their processes and procedures to efficiently process patients and ensure high quality of delivery. Our analysis of the outcome data clearly indicated that their efficiency and superior quality of service had resulted in a significant reduction in amputations for patients with certain ailments compared to their peers, thus improving the patients' quality of life and saving the agency and the government significant expenses for ongoing costs, had the amputations been performed. The answers lay in the data.

Our data analysts and data scientists collected and analyzed medical claims, mortality, demographic, census, health survey, and medical research, and other pertinent data from numerous sites, all part of the open data initiative launched by the federal government, including the Department of Health and Human Services (HHS), the National Institutes of Health (NIH), the Centers for Disease Control (CDC), Data.gov, and so forth.

Here's what we found:

- *Quality Matters:* Solving big data problems requires the use of multiple data sets from multiple data providers. Data consumers typically have no control over the quality of such data, nor are the data producers transparent about the data controls applied to the data set during creation. In this case, most of the open data initiative sites post disclaimers that no assumptions should be made regarding the validation and verification of the data that they are posting. This is a major issue, especially since these data sets are being used by policymakers and executives to make critical decisions impacting the well-being of millions of people.

- *Data Silo Challenge:* My team ran into data reconciliation issues when reviewing the same data from multiple data sources. The primary reasons for this are similar data residing in multiple silos and lack of data reconciliation across them. The team didn't know who to contact to resolve these issues or be the arbiter.

- *Governance and Controls:* Having the right data controls and governance processes in place is critical to ensure that the semantics and quality of the data are addressed and there is accountability within the producer organization. We weren't able to elicit much information regarding this from the data producers. This put tremendous strain on our resources, causing them to do due diligence and make critical assumptions regarding the quality and meaning of the data.

As the saying goes, *Garbage in Results in Garbage Out*[2]*;* hence, one cannot rely on analytical results based on data that is of poor quality. Many data sets that we analyzed were at the aggregate level, which masked issues with underlying detail-level data. For example, the coding of billing data from physician offices is very different from that of hospitals, since physicians usually perform procedures in outpatient settings, whereas hospitals tend to perform in inpatient settings.

When one looks at the aggregate-level data for a physician's outpatient charges, those charges seem high in comparison to those provided by the hospitals; the primary reason is the way individual items are coded from a billing perspective. Therefore, analyzing billing data across these two provider categories is not a straightforward process and is wrought with issues. The same is true for coding practices across physician offices, due to coding errors or transformations that occur within the electronic medical record (EMR) systems before they are transmitted to government agencies. One has to get inside the bowels of the data, understand it, analyze it, and connect the dots, before one can derive insights or reach conclusions. This is where the data scientists and subject matter experts step in.

The data quality, governance, and data reconciliation issues represent the other dark side of big data. They are very serious and have widespread ramifications to policy and business decisions. I would like to make the following recommendations to address these issues:

- *Data Certification:* Data producers certify the data that they produce and provide the data quality metrics, based on verification and validation checks.

- *Process Transparency:* Producers are transparent about the governance process undertaken.

- *Accountability:* Data producers must provide information about who is ultimately accountable for the governance and quality of the data being published.

- *Context:* Data producers should publish the contextual information related to the data, since data consumers have to process similar data (e.g., billing data or mortality data) from multiple sources and it helps to understand the context used by each producer. For example, entries should include the definition of each data element, the allowable values, the data types and quality checks, any aliases, and alignment with data standards.

---

*"Big data is only valuable
if it can be trusted."*

Cybersecurity is getting the most attention and investment lately, but it is equally important for federal, state, and local agencies and commercial enterprises to *invest in the quality of their data and their governance regimes.* Publishing massive amounts of data without the proper controls or process transparency puts a major strain on the consumers, who have to standardize, cleanse, normalize, and integrate the data based on incomplete contextual information, *putting the end result at risk.*

In the specific instance of our client, it behooves policymakers to use a holistic set of metrics and high quality data to evaluate health care providers, not just on billing data, but on *quality of care, efficiency of operations, quality of life improvements for the patients, and so forth.* This is the fair thing to do and will also incentivize care providers to do the right things, rather than to constantly look over their shoulders, worrying about Big Brother!

Five Takeaways and Action Items

1. The breadth of consumer data that is being acquired by the private and public sectors is vast. This puts an onus on the recipients to ensure that it is safeguarded and not misused.

2. The democratization and decentralization of data is providing greater opportunities for the bad guys to get their hands on sensitive and private data. The right safeguards must be implemented to prevent data leakage.

3. Another equally important aspect of the dark side of big data that doesn't get much publicity is its quality. Big data is only valuable if it can be trusted by consumers. As the saying goes, *Garbage in Results in Garbage Out;* hence, one cannot rely on analytical results based on data that is of poor quality.

4. Organizations are dealing with a highly fragmented data ecosystem. Therefore, they must ensure that data certification, process transparency, context, and accountability are in place. These are typically defined by the governance bodies and overseen at the enterprise level to ensure compliance.

5. Data producers have a responsibility to provide high quality data to their consumers. Publishing massive amounts of data without the proper controls or process transparency puts a major strain on the consumers, who have to standardize, cleanse, normalize, and integrate the data based on incomplete contextual information, putting the end result at risk.

PART THREE

Perils of Not Investing in Strategic Data Management

Chapter 10

Six Reasons Why Big Data Investments Aren't Paying Off for Some Organizations

Prospective clients always ask me if big data is a passing fad or something that's truly going to provide the benefits that they're looking for—deeper insights, better decision-making, and faster time-to-value. This is an important question that deserves an answer based on facts and not on marketing hype. In this chapter, I shall provide my perspective, but before I do that, I must state that big data is not a fad and will certainly benefit organizations, if it is implemented correctly.

According to a recent report, "Joining the Dots: Decision Making for a New Era,"[1] by the American Institute of CPAs (AICPA) and the Chartered Institute of Management Accountants (CIMA), *32 percent of 300 C-level executives at large organizations from sixteen countries around the world said big data had made things worse, not better, for decision-making.* In fact, 70 percent of those surveyed said at least one strategic initiative failed in the previous three years due to delays in strategic decision-making.

> *"32% of 300 C-level executives at large organizations from 16 countries around the world said big data has made things worse, not better, for decision-making."*

These findings fly in the face of the rhetoric heard around the industry. Before we go off and start finding fault with product vendors and industry pundits, let's take a step back and analyze the situation to identify the root causes for the current state of affairs.

Based on my experience with clients who have either made the leap into big data or have invested in proof-of-concept implementations, I've identified six reasons why big data investments aren't paying off for some of them: (1) lack of clear problem definition, (2) skill mismatch, (3) scope creep, (4) data wrangling challenge, (5) contextual gap, and (6) evolving technology.

Here's a deeper dive into each:

1. *Lack of clear problem definition:* Many organizations don't take the time to clearly articulate the problem(s) that they wish to solve with big data and to determine whether those problems truly need a big data solution. Picking the wrong problem, jumping in before clearly defining the problem, listing the questions that one wants to answer or a hypothesis that one needs to prove or disprove are recipes for disaster.

2. *Skill mismatch:* Hadoop and NoSQL implementations require a certain skill set, which is very different from traditional relational database skills. There is a tendency on the part of organizations to redeploy resources with traditional data skills to big data projects, before providing them adequate training in the frameworks, methodologies, and underlying architecture. This results in suboptimal designs and substandard products that may not meet the client's expectation. Under these circumstances, it is advisable to augment internal staff with big data specialists from service providers and big data product vendors.

3. *Scope creep:* Starting small and taking baby steps to reach the end goal should be the preferred approach. In order to test big data and prove its capability, it is best to start with a well-defined problem that has a narrow scope. This will provide an opportunity for the team (e.g., data analysts, data scientists, big data developers, and business domain experts) to stay focused and deliver results in a reasonable

amount of time. The end goal shouldn't be to test performance and scalability of the platform (that's a given), but to test the data ingestion, data wrangling, modelling, and analytics processes end to end.

4. *Data wrangling challenge:* For business customers, time-to-value is paramount. There is a tendency on the part of IT not to appreciate the time and effort required for wrangling data to get it right. Industry estimates put this at approximately 70 percent of the effort.

5. *Contextual gap:* Solving complex problems that are multi-dimensional in nature requires significant contextual data and business domain knowledge, in addition to the availability of large sets of raw data. This tribal knowledge isn't readily available in a repository but has to be extracted from various individuals. Given the siloed nature of organizations and their focus on parochial interests, this tends to have a major impact on project deliverables.

6. *Evolving technology:* It took relational databases a decade or two to mature and become robust enough to support business transactions. The same is true of big data technologies. Various components of the big data platform are evolving and maturing. It is important to keep this in mind as organizations embark on big data projects. Do the due diligence to determine which components of the big data stack are relatively stable and which ones aren't. Design your solution to take these data points into account, so that you reduce your dependency on the less-mature components or have alternate plans in case you run into issues. Leverage expertise provided by product vendors and integration partners.

I always advise clients to remember the maxim *Buyer Beware.* What is clear from the above is that organizations must perform the necessary due diligence before implementing big data. This will increase the probability of success and their ability to improve decision-making. All is not lost for organizations that have invested in big data and aren't seeing the desired results. I'd suggest they take a step back and consider the points made above, identify the bottlenecks or issues with their implementation, and take corrective action.

Senior leaders and HR departments must address the issue of skills mismatch across the business, technology, and operational roles at the line level. Managers play a key role in the success of big data projects. They must be trained and equipped to ask the right questions, make decisions related to architecture and design options, and be able to scope out and plan the engagements. One should not expect them to transition into this new role without adequate training and management support.

My observations and assessments were validated by a recent *Forbes* article[2] titled "Inside American Express' Big Data Journey," wherein Ash Gupta, president of Global Credit Risk and Information Management for AMEX, listed three challenges along the way: (1) Adoption of new and immature technologies required significant organizational adaptation and cultural transformation. Old processes became obsolete. New approaches required fresh skills and approaches; (2) AMEX needed to recruit new talent with skills in big data solutions and approaches. This challenge was complicated by the scarcity of big data talent and compounded by two additional factors: (a) the need to always understand "business context," which comes from experience, and (b) the tendency for millennial big data talent to continually seek new challenges, creating a retention challenge; and (3) Mr. Gupta cited the "marketing process journey," which he characterized as a process of continuous improvement intended to consistently refashion customer experience in a positive way. For American Express, this meant employing the same kind of "test and learn" techniques and learning-through-iterative-improvement approaches that the firm used in the past to refine its customer marketing models.

Big data projects introduce new paradigms, new processes, and nontraditional skills and require organizations to change the way they operate. Although technology and data play critical roles, one must not minimize the importance of organizational culture, senior level sponsorship, and an organization's appetite for change.

"Although technology and data play critical roles, one must not minimize the importance of organizational culture, senior level sponsorship, and an organization's appetite for change."

By employing best practices and lessons learned on big data implementations, organizations can take proactive measures to increase the probability of success. They should also focus on implementing a "test and learn" methodology to improve their processes over time, resulting in better outcomes. The Big data talent gap must be tackled through in-house training and acquiring fresh talent.

Eight Takeaways and Action Items

1. Big data is not a fad and will certainly benefit organizations if it is implemented correctly.

2. One-third of the respondents to an international survey said that big data had made things worse, not better, for decision-making. 70 percent of those surveyed said at least one strategic initiative had failed in the previous three years due to delays in strategic decision-making.

3. We have identified six reasons why big data investments aren't paying off for some organizations: (1) lack of problem definition, (2) skills mismatch, (3) scope creep, (4) data wrangling challenge, (5) contextual gap, and (6) evolving technology.

4. What is clear from the above is that organizations must perform the necessary due diligence and get advice from firms such as AlyData before implementing big data.

5. Senior leaders and HR departments must address the issue of skills mismatch across the business, technology, and operational roles.

6. Managers play a key role in the success of big data projects. They must be trained and equipped to ask the right questions, make decisions related to architecture and design options, and be able to scope out and plan the engagements.

7. Big data projects introduce new paradigms, new processes, and nontraditional skills and require organizations to change the way they operate.

8. Technology and data play critical roles, but one must not minimize the importance of organizational culture, senior level sponsorship, and an organization's appetite for change.

Chapter 11

Leaders Uninvolved in Strategic Data Management Do So At Their Peril

"Data is the new electricity." - Satya Nadella

At a keynote in New York[1] titled "Data Is the New Electricity," Satya Nadella made a compelling case for data as a transformative force within organizations. He shared the impact technology and data are having on Microsoft's customers and their leaders.

Nadella discussed the concept of the Fourth Industrial Revolution[2] or the digital revolution, which has a broad and deep impact on our lives, and then talked about the causes of its transformative impact. He further discussed the confluence of circumstances that brought all this about—highlighting technology that connects everything - every person, place, and thing. These entities create lots and lots of data, he continued, in the zettabytes. He mentioned the cloud as one of the components of the digital transformation *and stressed the fact that this is creating a tumultuous period of change for businesses.*

The slogan "Data is the new electricity" is profound! It's not just the data by itself that's important, but the process of being able to generate insights from data that matters most. That's what the Fourth Industrial Revolution is all about, concluded Nadella.

What are the frameworks of law? What are the enduring principles? How are you going to keep data secure? How is it going to stay private? How are users going to use this data? These are questions he posed to the audience. Complex questions that have to be tackled and may take many years for us to get our arms around them.

Think about this in the context of what data means to your organization and to you personally. It is the lifeblood of organizations and has to be generated and distributed to consumers, before it is put to meaningful use.

If you've read the previous chapters, you would have gathered that data is a strategic asset that organizations and leaders neglect at their peril. In this chapter, I will discuss the primary reasons why leaders aren't investing in SDM and how such decisions impact their organizations.

This particular topic is top of mind for me, since I recently met with the head of data and information quality at a multinational firm to discuss his company's data-related challenges. During the meeting, we discussed various topics, including the organization's culture and its senior leadership's views on SDM. The following statement made by the client caught my attention and struck a chord:

> *"Our senior leadership pays lip service to data management. They don't take data seriously."*

Upon returning to the office, I began jotting down some notes, based on my personal observations, and professional experience. Here are the five reasons I've identified concerning the lack of focus on data by leaders and their relatively low investment in SDM:

1. *Mind-set:* Leaders still have an information technology–centric mindset. In their minds, IT and strategic data management are synonymous, even though SDM is a specialized

field that has matured over the last two decades. I address this in the chapters *Welcome to the Dawn of Data, Who's on Point for Data, The Eleven Data Management Knowledge Areas,* and *Data Needs a Seat at the Table.*

2. *Lack of Awareness:* Leaders don't understand what strategic data management is, why they should invest in it, and why they have to become data savvy.

3. *Data is complex:* Data is pervasive and complex and managing it is extremely challenging. It is the job of SDM experts and data practitioners to demystify it, explain the emerging challenges faced by the organization due to big data and IOT, and explain how emerging frameworks and technology can be used to build new capabilities.

4. *Don't understand the benefits:* They haven't realized that IT is an enabler, but data is a weapon that can be a game changer. No one has shown them the positive impact that investments in SDM and analytics can have on the bottom line.

5. *Don't appreciate the risks:* The decentralization and democratization of data is introducing massive amounts of complexity and exposing organizations to legal, financial, and reputational risks.

We are in the midst of a historic shift that is forcing organizations to become data-driven. It behooves senior leaders, practitioners, and decision makers to become data savvy and to invest in SDM, so that data is managed as a strategic asset and that organizations gain deeper insights and are able to unleash its power.

Three Takeaways and Action Items

1. Our informal surveys indicate that there is a general feeling among the rank and file that senior leadership merely pays lip service to data management. They don't take data seriously. This perception needs to change if organizations are to become data-driven. Leaders have to lead by example.

2. We have identified five primary reasons for the lack of enthusiasm and investment in SDM from the leaders. They are (1) mind-set, (2) lack of awareness, (3) complexity of the data ecosystem, (4) lack of ROI, and (5) lack of risk awareness.

3. We are in the midst of a historic shift that is forcing organizations to become data-driven. It behooves decision-makers to become data savvy and to invest in SDM so that their organizations can stay competitive and not get disrupted.

PART FOUR

Who's Leading Your Data Function?

Chapter 12

The Politics of Data

> *"Information is power. But like all power, there are those who want to keep it for themselves." - Aaron Swartz*

Politics[1] plays a major role in how data is managed, governed, controlled, and distributed within firms. Organizational politics impacts critical decisions related to data management, influences the budget for data management functions, and determines whether data is treated as a strategic asset or just a byproduct of internal and external transactions.

The former head of operations and technology at Fannie Mae, Pascal Boillat, used to make a statement when things got rough and he wanted some answers to get to the root cause. He would ask us to "put the fish on the table." This forced us to get the good, bad, and ugly related to the topic under discussion on the table and hash things out.

So, in this chapter, I will take Pascal's lead and put the fish related to the politics of data on the table so that you can appreciate why data management is such a challenging space and why organizations are struggling to tame this beast.

Let me put the fish on the table:

- There are data fiefdoms within organizations that are preventing or disrupting the flow of information and causing serious damage.

- *Data is the new electricity:* It needs to be extracted, refined, and cleansed since organizations run on data.

- *Data is the raw material for creating information and information is power:* Those who acquire and own data can create information and gain power by default. This is why data fiefdoms are prevalent within organizations and why they tend to control access. Power corrupts and absolute power corrupts absolutely, so these fiefdoms should be dismantled.

- *Data is pervasive:* It resides on tablets, desktops, laptops, and servers in various forms within an organization's firewall and also in the cloud.

- *Data is complex:* It is hard to understand without context, can live in multiple states, and evolves over time.

- *Data is touched and transformed numerous times* as it moves through an organization's information supply chain, which increases the chances of data quality and consistency issues.

- *Data is a multichannel activity,* and it can be acquired through many channels and in a variety of formats,

- *Given the decentralization,* it's hard to set accountability for data.

- *Data requires context and subject matter expertise* that is dispersed around the organization.

- *Data is exploding* in volume and constantly evolving.

- *Data needs infrastructure and application support* to process, transform, and store it.

- *Data is fragmented* and usually sits in silos that may be owned by different departments.

- *Data management is an emerging field* that is gaining traction and maturity across organizations rather quickly.

- *Raw data is useless;* it needs enrichment, augmentation, and integration to be converted to information.

Leaders and staff should debate the following seven questions internally and bring the results to their leadership team's attention:

1. Who owns an organization's data? Is it owned by the heads of various departments? The shareholders? Someone else? These questions lie at the heart of the problems. Gaining clarity on this and laying out the organization's principles related to them should resolve the issues of data hoarding and data fiefdoms.

2. Should organizations assign a data czar or a CDO, with real authority and not just a title, to drive data-related standards and policies, governance, and quality and data management best practices? Do we need another C-level officer within the C-suite?

3. Should strategic data management (SDM) be split away from information technology (IT) and become a standalone function?

4. If SDM becomes a separate function, to whom should it report - departments in business, operations, or technology department?

5. Does the CDO have a seat at the C-level table and report to the chief executive or have a dual reporting structure to the CRO/CFO/COO/CIO and the CEO?

6. What should the CDO role be accountable for?

7. Should the CDO be a peer to the CIO or report to the CIO?

There are no simple answers to the questions above, since each organization is unique and has its own cultural dynamics. A model that works for one organization may not work in another. For example, highly regulated organizations such as those related to government, financial services, telecommunications, and healthcare need high quality data for risk management, regulatory compliance, decision-making, and analytics and, hence, are more apt to assign a CDO, while other industries may prefer to maintain the status quo and let the IT organization manage the infrastructure, applications, and data management functions.

The bottom line is that we are living in the age of big data and Internet of Things (IOT) and it behooves each company to ensure that data is treated as a strategic asset, data fiefdoms are eliminated, and data receives the right level of sponsorship, investment, and importance at the senior-most levels.

Three Takeaways and Action Items

1. Internal politics plays a major role with respect to data and data management within firms of all sizes. Organizational politics impacts critical decisions related to data management, influences the budget for data management functions, and determines whether data is treated as a strategic asset or just a byproduct of internal and external transactions.

2. Organizations and leaders that wish to become data-driven must put this fish on the table, debate it, and produce a clear set of policies to address these issues.

3. The seven important questions posed to the reader must be tackled, and the underlying issues must be resolved.

Chapter 13

Who's On Point For Data?

We are living in the age of big data[1] and IOT[2]. Strategic data management is an emerging field and it is gaining momentum quickly. Financial services and telecom verticals have embraced it and have made significant investments to mature their data management practices. Other verticals such as healthcare and public sector enterprises are lagging behind in terms of data management investment and maturity.

If you've been following my writings, you've realized that data is an organization's lifeblood, so it mismanages data at its peril.

During my data advisory engagements, my first order of business is to find out who is on point for data in the client's organization. Over the years, I've observed that the data function reports into various organizations—CEO, CFO, COO, CIO, CMO, or CRO. I've also encountered firms where no senior leader is assigned ownership of the data management function, which means it is owned jointly across multiple leaders. This is a major issue and sets the organization up for failure or serious challenges.

You are probably surprised by this revelation, especially since data is a critical function. We must start exploring the following questions to determine whether there are patterns or specific reasons for this:

- Why don't all organizations have a CDO/CAO or CDS role?

- Why doesn't the data function reside within the same C-level organization across all firms? and

- Why doesn't the CDO or the executive responsible for data management and analytics report directly to the CEO? CFOs are direct reports to the CEO and so are the CROs. This is typically not the case for the CDO or the C-level executive who is responsible for data.

For the purpose of the discussion going forward, I will use the CDO title to represent the data function and it will represent the CAO and CDS roles.

In my opinion, there are four reasons that are causing the inconsistent treatment of data across firms:

1. Data management is an emerging field, and *no one in the c-suite and at the board level really understands it well.* This results in it getting slotted within the organization that has the most data management challenges or is perceived to be the champion for data.

2. Data is pervasive and impacts every organization, and therefore it's hard to decide where to put it.

3. *It depends on the lens the board and the CEO apply.* If they apply a regulatory compliance or risk lens, they put it in the CRO's control. If they apply a profit-center lens, they put it in the CMO. If they apply a business operations lens, they put it in the COO's control. If they apply a finance and accounting lens, they put it in the CFO's control. And if they apply an IT lens, then it is slotted under the CIO.

To me, where the data function resides is not important, although I firmly believe that it will eventually be owned by a C-level executive, will be a direct report of the CEO, and will have the CEO and board's ear. What is most important is that the C-level executive who owns it, is data savvy, has excellent communication skills, understands the business domain, has strong influencing skills, and is given the authority and resources to get things done.

Where does the data organization reside within your firm and why? You should certainly look into this, develop your own points of view and share them with your management chain.

Not having the data function sit in a prominent position within the C-level hierarchy and run by a data-savvy C-level executive is most certainly impacting your firm's mission and its bottom line.

Five Takeaways and Action Items

1. Data management is an emerging field and it is gaining momentum quickly.

2. Some verticals have embraced it and reached a high level of maturity, while others are lagging.

3. Data is an organization's lifeblood, so it mismanages data at its peril.

4. In many organizations, data is managed in an ad-hoc manner, with no central authority defining standards and policies and driving governance or federating this out. This is not advisable since it exposes firms to risk.

5. The data function is not treated consistently across organizations for four reasons: (1) lack of understanding and appreciation of the field, (2) given the pervasive nature of data, it's hard to determine where authority should reside, (3) C-suite and board members determine the importance of this function, and (4) the leader of the data function must reside in the C-suite but companies aren't sure where.

Chapter 14

Six Facts That Determine whether Your Organization Needs a CDO

In the chapter titled *The Politics of Data,* I tackled this very complex topic and posed some questions to you, the reader. In this chapter, I will share the same six questions and provide some thoughts:

- Should organizations assign a data czar or a CDO, with real authority and not just a title, to drive data-related standards and policies, governance, and quality and data management best practices? Do we need another C-level officer within the C-suite?

- Should SDM be split away from IT and become a stand-alone function?

- If SDM becomes a separate function, to whom should it report—the business, operations, or technology departments?

- Does the CDO have a seat at the C-level table and report to the chief executive or have a dual reporting structure to the CRO/CFO/COO/CIO and the CEO?

- What should the CDO role be accountable for?

- Should the CDO be a peer to the CIO or report to the CIO?

The answers aren't simple, but I would like to share my thoughts based on my experiences at organizations across industry verticals.

Here are the six facts that you can use to determine whether your organization needs a CDO, a.k.a. The Data Czar:

1. Is your organization regulated or not? If you are a regulated entity, then it's best to designate or hire a CDO.

2. Are you a data-driven organization? By this, I mean are your management and staff highly dependent upon and passionate about data and do they use it extensively in their day-to-day operations? If the answer is yes, then you need a CDO.

3. Is a significant portion of your revenue derived as a result of data or by monetizing data? If yes, then you need a CDO.

4. Is data management becoming a drag on your bottom line, is data quality is an issue, or are you being written up by internal or external auditors for data-related issues? If yes, then you need a CDO.

5. Are you overwhelmed by the data deluge and struggling to cope with it? The answer is simple, you need a CDO.

6. Is your IT department struggling to deliver reporting, business intelligence, and analytics infrastructure and solutions that meet the business's needs? If yes, then hire a CDO.

Please note that a CDO can't perform miracles, but creating this role, and giving it authority and a reasonable budget, will enable your organization to leverage its data assets and overcome data management challenges.

Two Takeaways and Action Items

1. Have an internal debate within your organization to determine who is ultimately responsible for driving governance, quality, and data management.

2. If you aren't satisfied with how your data management functions are operating, then you should take steps to highlight the gaps and influence change.

Chapter 15

Some CDOs Are Thriving
While Others Are Departing - Here's Why?

The CDO role has gained lots of publicity and traction lately, especially within highly regulated industries such as financial services, healthcare, insurance, and the public sector. The White House has hired DJ Patil as the first chief data scientist, and several federal agencies and private sector corporations have hired CDOs over the last four or five years.

I read an article on Nextgov.com[1] that mentioned that three CDOs from US federal agencies had departed, and so have several CDOs from the private sector. I also learned that the UK government's first chief data officer Mike Bracken has departed. Many industry publications have labeled it the sexiest role in the industry. If that is true, then why are CDOs leaving in large numbers? Is it by personal choice, for better opportunities, or for lack of appreciation and support? I was compelled to write this chapter to shed some light on the role and the challenges CDOs face in trying to stay relevant within the c-suite and add value to their respective organizations.

In order to understand why some CDOs are thriving while others are barely surviving or are leaving their jobs, one must focus on four fundamental factors: value proposition, clarity of role, reporting structure, and sponsorship from the top. I have a feeling that the recent departures from the federal agencies and other organizations were due to one or more of these organizational factors:

- *Unclear CDO Value Proposition:* Lack of appreciation for and clear understanding of the strategic value of data and data management at all levels of the organization, especially at the top tiers.

- *Suboptimal Reporting Structure:* Does the CDO function belong in the business or the technology domain? And was he or she reporting into the right organization?

- *Lack of Clarity of the Role:* Many organizations lack a clear definition of the CDO's role and responsibilities vis-à-vis the CIO and CTO roles.

- *Lack of Sponsorship and Support:* Managing and governing data across organizational silos is a demanding and complex task. Was the CDO provided top-level cover, sponsorship, support, and adequate budget to scale the organization and build a strong team of data management experts who could drive change across the organization? Was there an appreciation for the hard work required?

I will address each of the four organizational factors and provide my assessment of the situation.

1. **CDO Value Proposition**

Jane Snowdon, IBM's chief innovation officer for federal agencies, says that the three big fundamental shifts happening in government today—cloud, mobility, and citizen engagement—are all dependent on data. A 2015 report from IBM's Center for Applied Insights[2] found that 61 percent of the 250 CIOs surveyed at large organizations wanted their employer to recruit a CDO in the next year.

Many organizations jump on the CDO bandwagon before clearly articulating the value that this role brings in terms of addressing data-related issues, gaining better insights from data, streamlining data management processes, reducing costs, and so forth. If an organization hasn't done due diligence and can't clearly articulate the value of the role and the opportunities it presents, it shouldn't move forward with the hiring process.

In the chapter titled *The Eleven Data Management Knowledge Areas,* I list the individual data management knowledge areas. It will help you to understand why data management is a specialized field requiring very specific knowledge, skills, and expertise and, therefore, requires a leader who is not just aware of the knowledge areas, but has practical experience leading enterprise-wide data management programs, has deep business domain knowledge, and has strong influencing skills.

2. The CDO Role and Responsibilities

Defining the CDO, the responsibilities associated with it, and how it is different from the CIO and CTO roles is extremely important if organizations want to build a data-driven culture.

Much of the work of people who are pioneering CDO positions at big bureaucracies remains necessarily "remedial," as the UK's first CDO Mike Bracken states. That means, "finding out where data is, what contracts govern it, how it can be used, what standards it's in, and getting it out of legacy IT systems," Bracken says.

As a data practitioner, a student of strategic data management, and someone who reported directly to the CDO of the largest financial services firm in the world, I experienced and witnessed these challenges in real life. In the 2004 to 2008 timeframe, executives with stellar backgrounds and impressive data management credentials were hired for the role when it wasn't dubbed CDO, but "head of enterprise data management" or "head of enterprise data governance." Most were unsuccessful in their endeavor for various reasons, mostly having to do with the politics of data or the organization's inability to clearly articulate what the position's role and responsibilities were vis-à-vis the head of IT (i.e., CIO). The overlap in functions between the CIO and CDO roles, a dependence of the data management executive on the CIO for infrastructure and technical execution, and turf wars were critical factors that played into this.

After the crash of 2008[3], new regulations, such as Dodd-Frank[4], Solvency[5], and BASEL[6], forced many organizations to focus on data governance, data and information quality, and consolidation of master data to better manage risk and improve regulatory compliance and analytics. This focus on data governance and management caused organizations to introduce a new C-level executive into the C-Suite and, hence, the "head of enterprise data management & governance" title was renamed "chief data officer."

Some organizations were eager to impress regulators, while others felt introducing a CDO into the C-Suite would show internal and external stakeholders that data was finally getting the focus it deserved. The jury is still out on whether these moves have made a difference with respect to gaining better insights from data, managing data in a more efficient manner, understanding business-critical data, or reducing complexity in obtaining data from various data silos.

In order to get to the right answer with respect to a CDO's role and responsibilities, here are some questions that must be addressed:

- Should the CDO focus only on data strategy and governance, or should he or she be responsible for analytics as well?

- If the CDO is responsible for analytics and insights, then does this translate into building a center of excellence, the technical capabilities, and execution team, in addition to the strategy and governance aspects?

- Is the CDO role purely an advisory and evangelist role, or does it involve solution development and technical execution as well?

- Is the CDO a change agent with a transformation agenda and enforcement powers, or purely a figurehead with a mandate to develop enterprise data standards and policies?

- Data and technology are intertwined, so how does the CDO role differ from that of the CIO? Should there be joint accountability for data between the two roles to encourage collaboration?

- What are the role and responsibilities of the CIO vis-à-vis the CTO?

- Is the CIO still relevant in the new world of cloud computing and outsourced shared services models or has the role diminished? Can the CIO role be merged with that of the CTO?

- Can the CIO, whose primary focus has been on infrastructure and technology execution, transform himself or herself and take on the CDO function as well? Are the skills, business domain knowledge, and experience required for both the roles identical or are there differences?

- A controversial yet important consideration: Should organizations morph the CIO role into the CDO role rather than introduce a new C-level executive into the C-suite?

Each organization is unique with respect to its culture, data, and IT ecosystems, as well as level of IT and data maturity, so thorough analysis and an internal debate among the senior leadership team members is necessary to get to the best definition of the CDO's role and responsibilities.

Once the role and responsibilities of the CDO are clearly defined and agreed upon by the C-suite and the board, the next step is to finalize the reporting structure and the budget.

3. Reporting Structure

The reporting structure defines the corporate pecking order, span of control, and in some cases gives credibility to a particular role within an organization. In "Politics of Data," I address the on-the-ground political realities that I've observed and experienced at large organizations. This must be taken into consideration while defining the CDO reporting structure.

Business departments have a vested interest in ensuring that they can trust their data and that it is properly managed. Therefore, data management practitioners feel data governance, data requirements, and accountability belongs within the business areas, but business hasn't really embraced this notion and is yet to take accountability for business-critical data. That transition needs to occur before the CDO function gains recognition and importance. Business organizations must embrace data management, educate themselves about the field and associated best practices, and become custodians of their data.

If data belongs in the business department, then CDOs must report into the business department, be the evangelist for data management, and champion the cause of data on behalf of the business, and work closely with their technology counterparts to execute on the strategy, governance, and analytics.

4. Sponsorship and Support

Strategic data management programs aren't projects with fixed start and end dates. They are multiyear initiatives that require sponsorship, funding, and political backing since they must transform organizations by forcing a data-driven culture, enforcing standards and policies, implementing robust data governance, and introducing new tools and technologies.

My Recommendations

I don't like raising issues without offering solutions. Based on personal experience, and having weighed the pros and cons of various models currently in use within organizations that I've advised, here are a few recommendations:

- As organizations adopt the cloud, and outsource development and support via internal and external shared services groups, there's an opportunity for them to rationalize the C-Suite and potentially convert the CIO role into the CDO role, to shift the focus from infrastructure and technology to data management, data governance, and analytics. The CTO role should continue to focus on technology and R&D.

- Business departments must take ownership for corporate data and its governance and become its custodians. This is a prerequisite for the success of the CDO role.

- The CDO should report into the business department (CFO, CRO, COO, CEO, etc.), with a dotted line to the board (e.g., audit committee).

- The CDO role should be a peer of the CIO/CTO roles, so that he or she can stay objective and independent from the technology function with respect to decision-making and addressing data-related issues. Each of these roles has dependencies on the other; hence, very close coordination and cooperation are required between them to successfully execute against corporate goals.

- The CDO must be given a substantial budget and board-level support in order to be able to scale the organization and deliver against the key data management priorities, especially those related to data governance, analytics, risk management, and regulatory compliance.

The CDO role is a critical one and can transform an organization and drive tremendous value. However, the success or failure of a CDO isn't necessarily tied to just the capability of the person in the seat; there are additional organizational factors that influence a CDO's tenure and effectiveness. These are: (1) clarity of the role and responsibilities, (2) realistic expectations, (3) strong support and sponsorship from the top, (4) adequate multiyear investment, (5) where and who the CDO reports into, (6) whether the business department is willing to own and become the custodian of the data, and (7) a culture that is willing to change and adapt to the new realities of cloud computing, big data, IOT, data visualization, data mining, machine learning, and artificial intelligence.

"A CDO can transform an organization and drive tremendous value, provided he or she is given the necessary backing and support from leaders in the business and technology departments."

Six Takeaways and Action Items

1. The CDO role has gained lots of publicity and traction lately as organizations realize the value of data and the fact that they need a C-level leader to drive the data program forward.

2. Organizations are actively seeking out internal and external candidates to promote into the CDO role but are having trouble clearly articulating the scope of this executive's role and determining the responsibilities he or she will be assigned. Many organizations jump on the CDO bandwagon before clearly articulating the value the role brings, and this has undesirable results.

3. Defining the CDO role and responsibilities associated with it, and how it is different from the CIO and CTO roles, is extremely important if organizations want to build a data-driven culture.

4. Organizations should focus on four areas when considering a CDO. These are: (1) CDO value proposition, (2) the CDO role and responsibilities, (3) reporting structure, and (4) sponsorship and support.

5. Have an internal debate within your organization to determine who is ultimately responsible for driving governance, quality, and data management.

6. A CDO can transform an organization and drive tremendous value, provided he or she is given the necessary backing and support from leaders in the business and technology departments.

PART FIVE

Dealing with Data Management Challenges

Chapter 16

Five Tips for Solving Every Data User's Frustration

I've been in far too many situations over the years where data users are frustrated, unable to get the data that they need, when they need it, and at the right level of quality to get their job done.

In this chapter, I will explore why this is the case and what organizations can do to address this very serious issue. *The last thing organizations need is frustrated, demoralized, and unproductive staff.*

Data users have a simple requirement of their Information technology and data management organizations:

"Give me the data that I need quickly, give it to me in the right format, in an integrated manner, and with the right level of quality. I need this to get my job done, and I'm in no mood to listen to any excuses and sob stories. Period."

Since they have aggressive deadlines and important business goals to meet, they really don't care about what it takes to fulfill this request.

Let's review and consider both sides of the equation:

- Data users can't be successful without good, quality, integrated, and timely data.

- IT and data management organizations want to fulfill requests, but are hampered by many constraints—limited budgets, too many requests in the pipeline, fragile legacy systems, and lack of resources that have data management skills. The lack of credibility with end users doesn't help either.

There are numerous reasons why data sources can't be identified, why it's hard to understand the context within which data is used, why its quality is hard to manage, and why organizations are struggling. The primary ones are:

- Lack of an organization-wide data inventory or catalog

- Lack of accountability for data

- Missing contextual information

- Lack of organization-wide data quality standards and policies

There are no easy solutions to this quandary, but let me share my insights and five tips that organizations can use to address the situation (note: The terms in parentheses are the equivalent data management terms):

1. *Inventory (Catalog):* The first thing that needs to be done after receiving a request for data is figuring out where it lives. For this, organizations need a data inventory, which lists the systems of record and trusted data sources and the type and granularity of data each contains. For starters, a simple spreadsheet can get the job done, which can be migrated to a commercial tool after the associated data and processes are streamlined and agreed upon. This will expedite the data discovery process significantly.

2. *Accountability (Data Governance):* After you've located the data, you have to determine who is accountable for its operational maintenance and quality. This can be stored in the inventory database as well, at the data entity and/or data attribute level. The database will provide the IT and data management staff and end users visibility into who they must contact to address data related issues.

3. *Information Supply Chain (Supply Chain/Data Lineage):* In order to understand where data resides, you have to understand where it's been and where it's going. This can be accomplished by developing a diagram that depicts your organization's information supply chain (ISC). This isn't a simple task. It will require input from your IT, data, business, and operations teams, but it will pay dividends if you do it. Start at the highest level of the business, using your business architecture as a guide, and build the ISC in phases.

4. *Context (Metadata):* In order to understand data, end users need a lot of contextual information, such as its definition, format, allowable values, relationships, usage, and so forth. This should be captured in a data dictionary and glossary of terms. A simple spreadsheet is a good starting point, and you can migrate it to a commercial tool later.

5. *Quality (Data Quality):* As I have mentioned in this book, data quality is a foundational component of every organization's data management capability. In order to ensure the highest quality of data, organizations need to define the data quality dimensions that are important to them and then define quality requirements, measure quality, and address any issues proactively.

Data-driven businesses empower end users by providing self-service data discovery, business intelligence and analytics capabilities, transparency into the data ecosystem, access to rich contextual information, and education and training. Leaders have to drive this change.

A happy and productive staff tends to have a higher level of job satisfaction, are more innovative, and deliver better results, which directly improves the bottom line.

Four Takeaways and Action Items

1. Many data consumers are frustrated since they aren't able to get the data they need, when they need it, and at the right level of quality to get their jobs done.

2. It is important for leaders to recognize this and address the root causes for this frustration. The last thing organizations need is frustrated, demoralized, and unproductive staff.

3. Data-driven leaders should focus on the following five areas in order to reduce the level of frustration and drive user productivity. They are: (1) invest in a data inventory that will act as a catalog for enterprise critical data, (2) ensure that there is clear accountability assigned with respect to semantics, quality, and governance for all critical data assets, (3) provide some visibility into the ISC and data lineage, (4) for full understanding of data, end users need much contextual information, so leaders must invest in developing a centralized system to manage context (i.e., metadata), and (5) implement an enterprise data-quality program to develop standards and policies related to quality and drive the adoption of data quality best practices and the associated tooling into the organization.

4. End users of data should be empowered through self-service capabilities, transparency into the data ecosystem, access to rich contextual data, and investment in data management and data science education and training.

Chapter 17

It's High Time Business and IT Leaders Unite

> "Business is from Mars, IT is from Venus."
> – Author's quote

I n many organizations, IT is responsible for not just technology but data management too. Therefore, as service providers to the business departments, IT staff work closely with business teams to deliver on mission-critical systems. Unfortunately, my experience has been that the relationship between IT and business departments is usually strained and in some cases completely dysfunctional. IT lacks credibility with the business department, and this builds tension and a trust deficit.

For organizations to flourish and stay competitive, IT and business departments must set aside their differences and unite so that they can operate as a single entity, not two separate departments with separate sets of priorities and an inability to communicate with each other.

Men Are from Mars, Women Are from Venus was written in 1993 by relationship counsellor John Gray. Over the years, it has sold over fifty million copies and spent 121 weeks on the bestseller list. The book states that the most common relationship problems between men and women are a result of fundamental psychological differences between the genders, which the author exemplifies by means of its eponymous metaphor: that men and women are from distinct planets—men from Mars and women from Venus—and that *each gender is acclimated to its own planets society and customs, but not to those of the other.*

I took the liberty of replacing "Men" with "Business" and "Women" with "IT" and developed a new phrase - "<u>Business Is from Mars, IT Is from Venus.</u>"

I hope I'm not going to get into trouble with John for modifying his phrase, but I'll take my chances since my intentions are noble.

Just to clarify, "Business" refers to the business department(s) and "IT" refers to the information technology department in a company.

During the span of my professional career, I have worked with and consulted at organizations of various sizes, from global Fortune 500 companies to private thirty-person operations. One thing has stuck with me and has kept nagging me over the years. *It was the realization that there is a major disconnect between business and IT departments in most organizations, regardless of their size or the business domain they operate in. In fact, in many cases the relationship is so bad that it borders on being dysfunctional.* This has serious ramifications for the organization, since each of these departments plays a critical role in running and changing the business to achieve strategic goals.

Why am I writing about overcoming the business-IT divide, you may ask? It is because the data folks are usually stuck in the middle of the business and IT teams and are impacted by the business-IT divide.

After analyzing this problem from various angles, I've identified six reasons for the disconnect between business and IT. Here they are:

1. *They speak different languages:* Business speaks shareholder value, bottom-line results, and top-line growth. IT speaks cloud, servers, cybersecurity, and networks.

2. *There is a trust deficit:* Business cares about time-to-value, but IT cares about infrastructure, applications, and keeping things running smoothly.

3. *There is a misalignment of goals:* Usually business and IT goals aren't in alignment, making it hard for them to satisfy each other's needs.

4. *The incentives aren't right:* Typically, business and IT are incented differently—business on profitability and shareholder value, IT on keeping the train running.

5. *They each have challenges and constraints that hold them back:* Business is dealing with competitive challenges and aggressive goals, and IT is challenged by legacy systems, limited budgets, and a very dynamic landscape.

6. *They come from very different worlds:* Business teams typically have limited or zero understanding of technology and its implementation, and IT typically has limited or zero understanding of the business domain, all of which makes it difficult to get things done.

Here's my simple solution to this conundrum:

> *"Have business and IT swap seats for a day.*
> *Ask each of them to deal with the minute details*
> *of running the other's departments*
> *and making tough decisions,*
> *based on limited data and budgetary constraints."*

This exercise will give both parties an appreciation for the other's goals, domains, constraints, and challenges and bring them closer, since it helps to walk a mile in someone else's shoes. Where there is a will there is a way! In addition, it is important for leaders from each department to overcome their differences and come together for the good of the organization.

As part of her research agenda at Gartner, Valerie Logan is focused on the increasing diversity of data and analytics professionals and leaders, and the resulting gap in effective communications, and "shared language". With a broad array of rookies and veterans, business and IT heritage, and rapidly emerging data sources, solutions, and technologies, the need for a recognized common language could not be greater. She is also focused on serving the needs of emerging CDOs, and CAOs as the cadre of master change agents focused on teaching, translating, and guiding organizations in their leverage of data as a strategic asset.

Five Takeaways and Action Items

1. The relationship between IT and business departments is usually strained and in some cases completely dysfunctional. IT lacks credibility with the business department, and this builds tension and a trust deficit.

2. "Business Is from Mars, IT Is from Venus," which implies that they aren't compatible. This has serious ramifications for the organization since each of these departments plays a critical role in running and changing the business to achieve strategic goals.

3. For organizations to flourish and stay competitive, IT and business departments must unite and operate as a single entity, with goals, incentives, and priorities aligned.

4. The six reasons for the disconnect between business and IT are: (1) they speak different languages, (2) there is a trust deficit, (3) there is a misalignment of goals and priorities, (4) the incentives aren't right, (5) they each have challenges and constraints, and (6) they come from very different worlds.

5. One solution for addressing the relationship challenges is to have business and IT staffs swap roles for a day or two. This will give each team an appreciation for the other's challenges and constraints and, hopefully, bridge the gaps.

PART SIX

Building a Data-Driven Company

Chapter 18

Six Key Ingredients for Building a Data-Driven Company

Let me share the story of a company that has built a multibillion-dollar business by monetizing data and analytics. It has developed a highly sophisticated data analytics platform that captures, processes, and analyzes massive amounts of data and distributes the results to thousands of clients worldwide, across numerous verticals such as financial services, banking, advertising, healthcare, retail, telecom, and travel. For privacy reasons, I'll call this company the "Data-driven Enterprise"[1] going forward.

"Data-driven Enterprise" is a global leader in digital media analytics. It makes audiences and advertising more valuable to clients by providing trusted, independent metrics that help businesses understand how people interact with content and advertising across TV and digital devices, giving a total view of the consumer. Through its products and services, it helps its more than 2,000 clients understand their multiplatform audiences, know if their advertising is working, and access data where they want and need it. The company captures and analyzes over 1.5 trillion global interactions per month in order to gather insights and develop targeted metrics for its clients.

The chief technology officer of "Data-driven Enterprise" is a good friend of mine. Since I wanted to ask him about the key ingredients that have driven his company's success and its ability to create a multibillion-dollar data-driven business, I interviewed him for this book.

The six key ingredients for success that he shared with me are: (1) foster a startup culture, (2) always focus on customers' needs, (3) constantly innovate, (4) pay attention to changing market conditions and adjust, (5) build a robust data platform, and (6) ensure complete alignment on goals and incentives between the business and information technology organizations.

To provide additional insights, let me elaborate on each of the six ingredients.

1. **Foster a startup culture**[2]: The maxim *"Culture trumps Strategy"* is tried and tested. As startups grow, their culture tends to change for the worse. Pressure added from shareholders and the board plays into this. Culturally, "Data-driven Enterprise's" management has been good at setting the vision and corporate goals and pushing them down to the rank and file, which has kept departments focused.

> *"Data-driven Enterprise has been able to maintain a culture where Return on Investment (ROI) isn't always the main driver when making decisions."*

It's incorporated a culture where associates learn from their data and drive directional efforts from it. An example of this is a brand new project, which started off as an effort driven by internal insights and gained dramatic market share in the ratings business.

2. **Always focus on customers' needs:** The firm's associates observed that clients were using data in either of two key points in the life cycle of the advertising use case, in the planning stage or the post-evaluation stage. They saw an opportunity in the middle and proceeded to build out technology that could measure every event from a page view perspective. They subsequently created a product that provided valuable page view metrics to clients on a daily basis. In order to validate whether a person did see an advertisement in the right country, the product was enhanced to provide that information as well. This enabled the client to ensure that the customer they set

at the planning stage was actually seeing the advertisements. This product also enabled customers to evaluate performance while a campaign was running and make in-flight optimizations to increase ROI and stay within its advertisement budget.

3. **Constantly innovate**[3]: So what's the company's secret sauce? It's empowering associates to take an idea and execute it and to create new data-driven products and new lines of business.

"Data-driven Enterprise focuses on innovation, combined with execution excellence—people, skill, culture, and its technology platform."

Over the years, its innovative culture and staff empowerment has resulted in the creation of several new products and new lines of business, which have consistently improved the company's bottom line.

4. **Pay attention to changing market conditions and adjust to them**[4]: In the early 2000s, this company identified a threat—the Internet had changed. The Internet went from being a single personal computer to multiple devices, shared use, and so forth. "Data-driven Enterprise" had to adapt to the change in the market to measure it. It asked clients to add a piece of code on their webpages; 90 percent of US media properties participated, resulting in an increase from one hundred billion data points per month to 1.5 trillion data points per month. This took a few years to implement across its customers' sites. It then built data assets of all events that they were capturing, and it determined that new products could be created, based on these data assets.

"Without the rich data, true insights wouldn't be possible. The firm also focused on identifying outliers and specific insights on buying behavior on the web that would tell a story to their customers."

---

5. **Build a robust data platform**[5]: The firm implemented a combination of a popular Hadoop distribution in 2011 and a Massively Parallel Processing (MPP) database offering for SQL access in 2010. This bifurcation between processing in MPP and Hadoop was done for latency reasons. The MPP platform provides the business team with easy access to data via SQL and business intelligence tools as soon as it's sourced from various channels.

The "Data-driven Enterprise" leverages the same infrastructure in the capture and processing of data across all its channels as well as internally and routes the results to the MPP and Hadoop platforms. In order to speed time-to-value, its business users use the same infrastructure as IT and have direct access to rich data sets.

A big change that IT made a couple of years back was implementing Agile Scrum.

"Agile execution methodology has kept information technology teams focused on product."

The "Data-driven Enterprise" uses cloud services like Akamai for the high transaction counts. For performance reasons and to achieve better control of its data, it doesn't run everything in the cloud, but uses colocation facilities as well.

6. **Ensure that business and information technology organizations are completely aligned:** Typically, IT is treated as a cost center, but at "Data-driven Enterprise," this is not the case. Therefore, pressure to reduce costs isn't a major driver. Technology is considered part of a single cross-functional team, since much of what the company does can't be accomplished without technology.

> *"'Data-driven Enterprise' is a technology and data analytics company that does research and provides metrics to its customers. Technology and deep analytics are part of its differentiation."*

Business and IT are completely aligned and operate in cross-functional teams. It's not just development teams working on a product; they also have analysts, data scientists, and product management staff working together and operating against a common set of goals. Incentive structures are based on revenue targets per product.

The "Data-driven Enterprise" sets revenue and expense targets from a goal perspective, so all business and technology heads are focused on how they create products and how they create growth. This keeps them aligned on the end goals and business priorities.

> *"Data is the new electricity. Advances in technology and data science have made it possible to create multibillion-dollar data-driven businesses."*

I'd advise corporate leaders to take a close look at a very strategic asset: data. The time is right for organizations to diversify their revenue streams by monetizing data. This will require fostering intrapreneurship within their ranks and focusing on the *Six Key Ingredients for Success* discussed in this chapter.

Five Takeaways and Action Items

1. Research has proven that companies that are data-driven are more successful than their peers are. In addition, there is an opportunity for them to diversify their revenue stream by monetizing data.

2. It is possible to create a multibillion-dollar business or a line of business within an organization by monetizing data and analytics.

3. The six key ingredients for a successful data-driven organization are: (1) foster a startup culture, (2) always focus on customers' needs, (3) constantly innovate, (4) pay attention to changing market conditions and adjust, (5) build a robust data platform, and (6) ensure complete alignment on goals and incentives between the business and information technology organizations.

4. Many organizations don't realize that they possess a very valuable asset—data—which, if managed well and used to generate valuable insights through analytics, can create a competitive advantage for them. In addition, there is an opportunity for them to diversify their revenue stream by creating data products or by selling highly enriched data to other organizations. In the chapter titled *Welcome to the Dawn of Data*, I share some examples of companies that have done this successfully.

5. Since it presents a few challenges to traditional organizations, becoming data-driven will require a major transformation internally. Increasing data literacy at all levels of the organization, creating a culture that values data and asks the right questions with respect to the data it uses,

building data science capabilities to extract deep insights from data, and using Agile methodologies to implement data projects are all crucial.

Chapter 19

Use Data Visualization to Tell Stories and Gain Influence

"A Picture is Worth a Thousand Words." – English Idiom

W e live complicated lives - at home and at work. We are inundated with a constant stream of data and information - and forced to make quick decisions, while we multi-task. Angelika Dimoka, director of the Center for Neural Decision Making at Temple University, conducted a study[1] that measured people's brain activity while they addressed increasingly complex problems (i.e., noise). As people reach information overload, Dimoka explained, "They start making stupid mistakes and bad choices because the brain region responsible for smart decision making has essentially left the premises." *Research also shows that the human brain can only deal with seven pieces of information at any one time and it is literally impossible for our brains to multitask (10 Surprising Facts About How Our Brains Work[2]).*

Based on these facts, it is clear that most of the decisions we make, aren't being made under ideal conditions. I'll let you draw your own conclusions of the implications of this research and how it impacts your personal and professional lives.

In general, the left hemisphere of our brain is dominant in language: processing what you hear and handling most of the duties of speaking. It's also in charge of carrying out logic and exact mathematical computations. When you need to retrieve a fact, your left brain pulls it from your memory.

The right hemisphere is mainly in charge of spatial abilities, facial recognition, and processing music. It performs some math, but only rough estimations, and comparisons. *The brain's right side also helps us to comprehend visual imagery and make sense of what we see.* It also plays a role in language, particularly in interpreting context, and a person's tone.

There are two challenges we have to deal with that require both hemispheres of our brains:

- Make important decisions quickly, based on lots of data and information, across many dimensions (e.g., time, space, business domains, subject areas, geography, historical facts, etc.).

- We have to use data and information to create visualizations that lead to interesting insights. These insights can be woven into a story and used to support or justify our decisions and to gain buy-in from others. Raw data and bits of information can't talk or tell a story. Just like a painter uses various color palettes to create shapes and forms on a blank canvas, to convey her complex ideas, we have to paint a picture for the audience.

Visualizing data and complex relationships is our best bet to simplify things and tease out important insights. This is a three step process, after we have prepared the data for analysis:

1. Present the information visually, to simplify the comprehension of data and relationships across the data.

2. Synthesize the data and ensure that we are able to summarize the key insights to seven or less.

3. Provide an interactive what-if analysis capability, to uncover the unknown/unknowns, which we wouldn't uncover, if the data were presented in a different manner.

You can start this process with a goal or a hypotheses and use data and information to lead you to it or just go through the exercise and let the insights gleaned from it, help you build your story and make important decisions.

The visualization below depicts the expenditure of the various U.S. Intelligence Agencies against 4 spending categories (1) Data Collection, (2) Data Processing and Exploitation, (3) Data Analysis and Management, and (4) Facilities and Support. Accordingly, to the designer of the graphic, "Data collection" involves gathering raw information, surveillance, satellites, human intelligences, etc. that are then exploited and analyzed. And "Management" handles these tasks.

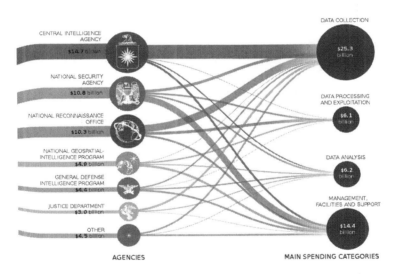

Figure 19.1 The Top-Secret U.S. Intelligence 'Black Budget' *(Diagram courtesy Martin Grandjean[3]).*

Imagine how difficult it would be to determine the breakdown of expenses by agency, if this data were presented in a tabular format.

The density of the lines is directly proportional to the expense for that category and the shaded areas represent the various agencies. This picture tells us that the CIA spends a significant portion of its budget on "Data Collection," a large portion of NSA's budget goes toward "Management, Facilities and Support," followed by "Data Collection," and the National Reconnaissance Office spends approximately half of its budget on "Data Collection."

In addition to this, we can also visualize that the highest expense across the agencies is on the "Data Collection" category (48%), followed by "Management, Facilities and Support" (12.5%), "Data Processing and Exploitation" (12.5%), and "Data Analysis" (27%).

These ratios align with the industry estimates of 70% to 80% spent on "Data Collection, Processing, and Preparation," and 20% to 30% on "Data Analysis".

If I were a decision maker running these agencies, I'd set aggressive goals to reverse this trend - spend a bulk of the effort and budget on "Data Analysis" to derive insights and significantly reduce the "Data Acquisition, Processing and Management" costs, by introducing automation, data quality rule re-use, pre-built data processing libraries, and other data management best practices.

Here's a visualization that tells a different story –

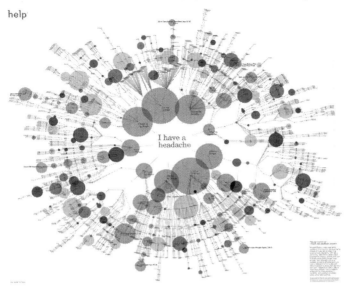

Figure 19.2 Infographic Visualizing Options for
Headache Medication *(Source: Help Remedies[4])*

This infographic depicts the options consumers are pre-sented with when they visit a drugstore looking for medicine to treat their headache. The main point it's trying to convey is that drug store aisles are now an eye-melting maze of choices, with products advertising everything from time-release to gel-caps, to flavors to different dosages. I guess this is the pharmaceutical industry's ploy to get us to buy different types and formulations of headache medicines - based on our age, brand preference, dosage, etc.

This happens to be an advertisement for *Help Remedies,* a startup that provides single-use packets at pharmacies labeled with the symptoms. (i.e., "I have a headache" or "I have allergies" or "I have a blister"). The chart does tell an interesting story about what innovation can do to a market at large. *Help Remedies* realized how complex finding medication for a relatively simple symptom such as headache was and turned it into a product that was easy to find on the shelf and would provide quick relief.

I didn't know how complex the decision making process for a simple medical symptom was, until I saw this visualization and read the story behind it. Isn't this ingenious? Critical insights that weren't visible before were only made possible via the visualization. The same concept can be applied to any industry and any complex problem.

These infographics and visualizations are certainly very impressive, but don't forget that acquiring the data, cleansing it, and preparing it, takes up a bulk of the effort. This is a pattern that I see across all the projects I'm involved with. *The key takeaway is that organizations have to invest in reducing the cost and effort required in the data preparation and cleansing steps.*

There are numerous open source and commercial products available on the market that provide the visualization capabilities described above. I've listed a few in the Appendix. I suggest you take a sample data set and visualize it using an open source tool to get the fundamentals right and try different design techniques. You may even uncover insights and discovery relationships from the visualizations that you wouldn't have otherwise (also known as unknown/unknowns). Once you've learnt the fundamentals and design techniques related to visualization, use them at work to influence your peers and the management team.

If you need additional inspiration, you can view David McCandless's TED talk on the beauty of data visualization[5] or JoeAnn Kuchera-Morin's new way of seeing, hearing and interpreting scientific data.[6]

To become data-driven, start visualizing your data and use it to tell stories. You will become influential within your organization and gain immense credibility with your peers and senior management.

Seven Takeaways and Action Items

1. Research shows that the human brain can only deal with seven pieces of information at any one time and it's literally impossible for our brains to multi-task.

2. As people reach information overload they start making stupid mistakes and bad choices because the brain region responsible for smart decision making has essentially left the premises.

3. There are two challenges we have to deal with that require both hemispheres of our brains (1) Make important decisions quickly, based on lots of data and information, across many dimensions, and (2) We have to use data and information to create visualizations that lead to interesting insights.

4. Visualizing data and complex relationships is our best bet to simplify things and tease out important insights. Critical insights that weren't visible when data was presented in tabular format were only made possible via visualizations.

5. Infographics and visualizations are certainly very impressive, but acquiring the data, cleansing it and preparing it, takes up a bulk of the effort.

6. The bottom line is that organizations have to invest in reducing the cost and effort required in the data preparation and cleansing steps.

7. To become data-driven, start visualizing your data and use it to tell stories. You will become influential within your organization and gain immense credibility.

PART SEVEN

Demystifying Data Management

Chapter 20

The Eleven Data Management Knowledge Areas

The eleven knowledge areas[1] related to data management and the environmental elements[2] involved will be discussed in this chapter.

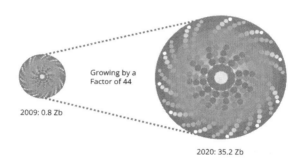

Growing by a
Factor of 44

2009: 0.8 Zb

2020: 35.2 Zb

Figure 20.1 Growth of Data

We are in the midst of a major transition from an IT-centric world to a data-centric one. I call this the Dawn of Data. Therefore, it is important that you are aware of the knowledge area framework and environmental elements of the field of data management. This will enable you to put things in perspective and understand how the various components of this framework fit and operate together.

Strategic data management is an emerging field that is fast gaining prominence and maturity. Understanding the framework and its implementation is extremely important for data management practitioners and non-practitioners alike.

Figure 20.2 Data Governance Wheel *(Source: DAMA)*

Figure 20.3 Data Management Goals and Principles
(Source: DAMA)

Figure 20.2 is called the Data Management Association Guide to the Data Management Body of Knowledge (DAMA-DMBOK) Framework wheel. It depicts the eleven major data management knowledge areas. Figure 20.3 depicts the environmental elements of a data management program (diagrams courtesy The Data Management Association).

As you will notice, similar to other fields such as information technology (ITIL, COBIT, CMMi, and ISO17799), the data management field uses a framework comprised of the following eleven knowledge areas, a data maturity model (DMM), and several specialized certifications (CDMP, CBIP, and DGSP):

1. data architecture

2. data modeling and design

3. data storage and operations

4. data security

5. data integration and interoperability

6. documents and content

7. reference and master data

8. data warehousing and business intelligence

9. metadata

10. data quality

11. data governance

Since data management activities occur within the context of larger engagements or as standalone projects, the following six environmental elements across the people, process, and technology dimensions have been defined:

1. organization and culture (people)

2. roles and responsibilities (people)

3. activities (process)

4. practices and techniques (process)

5. deliverables (technology)

6. tools (technology)

If you are interested in learning more about any of the knowledge areas, a *Data Management Book of Knowledge* (DMBOK) has been published by DAMA (http://www.dama.org). The website also provides a listing of the DAMA chapters worldwide.

Since developing solutions to complex data problems are daunting, I've defined a simple six-tier framework to clearly articulate how organizations should define and build the core components of their data architecture. This framework encapsulates the eleven knowledge areas described above. The six tiers are –

1. *Persistence tier* – SQL and NoSQL stores, Hadoop, etc.

2. *Transformation tier* – Transform and load data into the persistence tier

3. *Capability tier* – Data quality, context (i.e., Metadata), data catalog, security, and master and reference data

4. *Knowledge tier* – Combination of crowd sourced and manually entered data to capture institutional knowledge - knowledge related to the business critical data, business processes, and semantics

5. *Process tier* - Governance, authorization, issue management, configuration management, and data integration

6. *Insights tier* – Mine vast quantities of data to gain deep insights. Various industry terms for this are data science, machine learning, artificial intelligence, data mining, analytics, and business intelligence

Information about the Data Management Maturity Model (DMM) is available at http://cmmiinstitute.com/data-management-maturity. If you are interested in being certified in any of the specialized knowledge areas, the Institute for Certification of Computing Professionals (http://iccp.org) offers certifications, such as those for certified data management professional (CDMP), certified business intelligence professional (CBIP), and data governance and stewardship professional (DGSP).

Chapter 21

Data Governance Demystified—
Lessons From the Trenches

Data governance has become a top priority in the industry lately due to a renewed focus on big data, data security, data privacy, master data management (MDM[1]), reference data management, regulatory compliance, and data quality management. Many companies have some form of data governance[2] in place, via data controls (e.g., SOX controls[3]), structured development life cycle (SDLC[4]) checkpoints, design and code review boards, and architecture. However, these data controls and governance activities tend to lie within business silos and may not be handled consistently across all lines of business (LOB). Governing data across an enterprise in a standard and consistent manner is nontrivial, and companies frequently attempt it a few times before they get it right. Some of the reasons for the limited success are a corporate culture that is resistant to change, poor change management practices, lack of sponsorship from the top, lack of education about benefits of the program, scope creep, poor strategy and execution, or budgetary challenges.

Before embarking on a new program or addressing the deficiencies in an existing one, the following four fundamental concepts related to data governance must be understood and agreed upon by key stakeholders:

1. data ownership

2. accountability

3. organization

4. transparency

In addition, to ensure success, the following questions must be addressed at the outset:

- Which data entities and data elements should be governed at the enterprise level?

- What roles do the business, operations, and technology departments play in implementing data governance?

- What is the best model for data governance?

- What aspects of data should be governed?

- How should data-related issues be logged and addressed?

- How do organizations sustain data governance processes over the long haul?

Like any enterprise-wide initiative, there are no simple solutions to the data governance challenges faced by firms. However, if governing data is treated as a strategic priority and the data governance program is built systematically, sustainable data governance is achievable. While the overall strategy and execution steps will vary for each firm, based on the maturity of its data management practices and data governance processes (if initiated), the "data challenges" that it is facing, its appetite for change, the fundamental program-level components, and best practices that must be implemented remain the same.

Data-related Challenges

Data pervades every aspect of a firm's business ecosystem and is a strategic asset; therefore, it must be managed to deliver business value. The organic growth of data stores within corporations introduces challenges with respect to multiple definitions for a data element, multiple versions of the truth (i.e., lack of master and reference datasets), lack of integration of data between different data sources, inconsistent application of data security and privacy policies/standards, inconsistent data types and data precision, and lack of formality for governing data across the enterprise. The increasing rate of data acquisition, coupled with its complexity (structured and unstructured data—text, documents, graphics, video, audio, e-mails, social media feeds, and so forth), compounds this problem. Most firms are grappling with these challenges and trying to bring "order out of chaos." Investing in a data governance program or strengthening an existing one will enable them to overcome the challenges listed above.

Four Fundamental Concepts

Before embarking on a governance program or revamping an existing one, four fundamental concepts must be understood and bought into by key stakeholders.

1. Data Ownership

The question of data ownership is critical to governing data, since it deals directly with data accountability. If you ask the question "Who owns data?" across your firm, you will receive many interesting answers, including:

- Data producers own data.

- Data consumers own data.

- Business units that typically manage it (e.g., product lines) own data.

- The owner of the system where this data resides (system of record or trusted source) owns the data.

- The first system that receives the data and processes it owns it.

- The owner of the corporate data warehouse owns it.

You will discover that none of these answers is correct on an individual basis. Data is neither owned by a single business area nor an individual system owner, but is an enterprise asset that is owned by the corporation. However, to govern and manage data appropriately, organizations must identify and assign certain roles and responsibilities to staff members. Traditionally, roles such as data trustee, data steward, and data custodian have been used for this purpose. Some firms may choose to assign different titles to these roles—to better align with their organizational dynamics. These people are the frontline people who, likely, already make the key decisions regarding data. They need to be empowered to make the decisions, and their actions must be coordinated in such a way as to deliver business value.

2. Accountability

Having established the fact that data is a strategic asset owned by the corporation, three roles (or their equivalent) are typically defined: data trustee, data steward, and data custodian. These staff members play a critical role in governing data, in collaboration with other members within their organization. They should be empowered to make decisions and drive change and are ultimately accountable for ensuring that governance procedures are followed and their team members comply with enterprise data management policies and standards.

Data Trustee: A data trustee (officer-level staff member) is from the business or operations area and sits on one or more data governance boards. Data trustees are accountable for the security, privacy, data definitions, data quality, and compliance to data management policies and standards for a specific data domain. They collaborate with other trustees and the enterprise data governance team to define and approve data-related policies and procedures. Data trustees typically delegate the day-to-day data governance responsibilities to data stewards and data custodians within their organization.

Data Steward: Data stewards are subject matter experts in their respective data domains. They consult with and support business unit staff, the data trustee, and data custodians in their day-to-day data management responsibilities. Some of the data stewards' responsibilities are: defining data definitions, data security requirements, data privacy requirements, allowable values, and data quality requirements. Data stewards are also responsible for monitoring compliance to enterprise data management policies and standards, addressing data-related issues, and governing data belonging to their data domain. Data stewards also play a critical role in certifying the quality of data for their specific business domain.

Data Custodian: Data custodians (officer or director-level staff) typically belong to the information technology or operations area and manage access rights to data they oversee. In addition, data custodians implement controls to ensure the integrity, security, and privacy of their data. Data stewards and data custodians work closely to ensure that their organization complies with the enterprise data management standards and policies and that critical data-related issues are escalated to the appropriate data governance boards in a timely manner.

3. Organization

Data-related issues arise during the course of regular business. They could be related to data definitions, data consistency, data quality, alignment with industry standards, or a disagreement between business units on their use. All such issues should be captured and escalated from the local level (business unit) to one or more enterprise governance bodies for resolution. These governance boards are cross-functional and are typically composed of representatives of the business, operations, and technology teams. The specific number and structure of the governance councils will vary, depending on the size, culture, and preference of the firm's leadership.

4. Transparency

Complete transparency into data-quality-related and data-governance-related key value indicators (KVI) and key performance indicators (KPI), across the information supply chain, is essential for the success of a governance program. This provides two major benefits: first, measuring quality and process efficiency enables organizations to find and address material weaknesses; and second, providing every stakeholder a view into such metrics gives them the ability to not only become aware of hotspots and operational issues, but to have fact-based discussions about their impacts and resolutions with other stakeholders. It is uncomfortable for trustees, custodians, and stewards to have their dirty laundry aired in public, so expect some pushback. However, if they truly view data as a corporate asset and appreciate their role in proactively managing it, this should not be an issue.

The Mechanics of Governing Data

Having discussed the four fundamental aspects of governance, we have laid the foundation and can now discuss the mechanics.

1. Which data entities and data elements should be governed at the enterprise level?

To conduct business operations, enterprises consume and process thousands of data elements associated with dozens of data entities (e.g., product, party, customer, asset, payment, and orders). It is impractical to govern every data element; hence, focus should be on those that are deemed critical for business operations (e.g., financial reporting, various external disclosures, risk management, and accounting), decision making, and reporting purposes. It is necessary to engage subject matter experts within each line of business (e.g., product lines or functional areas) and corporate support function (risk, audit, procurement, customer support, finance, accounting, corporate reporting, and so forth) to identify the key business processes and the associated critical data elements. Focus must be on governing this set of enterprise critical data at the enterprise level, not on boiling the ocean.

Individual business units should set up local data governance organizations and data governance processes (utilizing the policies, standards, and procedures developed by the enterprise data governance team) to govern their line-of-business critical data. Local governance efforts should talk to one another in a stewardship council so that questions related to data ownership, data issues, and other such items can be settled.

To ensure ease of deployment and compliance to enterprise standards, LOBs should leverage the metadata, data quality, and compliance tools that are utilized by the enterprise data management team. If such tools are not available or there is no enterprise standard, then LOBs should engage with the appropriate enterprise team to evaluate and select them.

2. What roles do the business, operations, and technology departments play in implementing data governance?

In many organizations, IT tends to drive data governance or asserts that it should own it. Experience indicates otherwise. Business departments have a deeper understanding of data, its definition, and usage with respect to business operations, decision support, modeling, risk management, reporting the nuances of data from a semantic perspective, industry standards and alignment, and other such aspects. Business is also aware of the ramifications of data quality issues and inconsistencies in its application to the bottom line. Therefore, as subject matter experts, they should be assigned the role of data trustees and data stewards, with technology and operations teams playing a critical data custodian, trusted adviser, and implementation role, to ensure that the right systems, infrastructure, and processes are deployed to support and sustain data governance. This includes the capability to monitor compliance to data standards and policies, business intelligence into quality outliers and hotspots, data certification processes and underlying components, transparency into data inconsistencies, and data forensics' capability to analyze data and support root-cause analysis when issues are identified.

3. What is the best model for data governance?

This is an extremely important topic, on which the success of the program hinges. Governance should not be perceived as a Big Brother or a top-down program—stakeholders within business units resent this. A bottom-up approach, with the business units driving governance, doesn't work either, since business unit staff does not have a holistic view of data across the enterprise. A combination of top-down and bottom-up approaches works best. The industry term for this is *federated data governance*—an enterprise governance team facilitates the monitoring and management of the quality of enterprise critical data, with assistance from data stewards, data custodians, and data trustees from individual LOBs (top down). The business unit data stewards, data custodians, and data trustees govern LOB-critical data in collaboration with the enterprise governance team (bottom up). LOB-critical data is promoted to the enterprise critical data domain if there is consensus among all trustees that it belongs there.

4. What aspects of data should be governed?

Data-related issues mostly arise due to multiple and inconsistent data definitions (semantics) for a particular data element within data models or data stores, poor quality interface definitions that cause data corruption during data handoffs between systems, inconsistent data types, incomplete or inconsistent sets of allowable values for a data element, lack of basic data quality rules that must be applied, and the inability to trace the data element from a downstream system to its source. There are many other aspects of data that can be governed, but those are the more important ones. These are nontrivial issues and need a concerted effort to align the entire company to a centralized repository of the single version of the truth.

5. How should data-related issues be logged and addressed?

Proactive identification and management of data-related issues is required to lower systemic impacts. Each enterprise critical data element should be tagged with its system of record, trusted source, data custodian, data trustee, data steward, and other pertinent metadata to facilitate root-cause analysis and remediation of issues. Issues should be logged in an enterprise issue management system and assigned to the respective steward and custodian, whose role is to triage the issues, drive root-cause analysis, assign them to the appropriate owner (data, process, or technology), and ensure that they are resolved per agreed-upon service-level agreements. The enterprise governance team should mine issue-related data to find patterns of data anomalies, run some predictive analytics on the impact of such issues to downstream systems, and provide aging reports to management.

6. How do organizations sustain data governance programs over the long haul?

Because information governance is an emerging and evolving practice, you should plan on investing in education, and occasional checkpoints with one of the advisory firms that focuses on this niche. There is also a need to have the right people managing and coordinating data governance operations: strong senior analysts with business plus technology backgrounds and a customer orientation (customer here means the business stakeholders whose interests need to be furthered).

Lessons from the Trenches

A summary of the lessons that I learned while implementing data governance and data quality programs is provided below. This is not an exhaustive list, but I have attempted to capture items that I felt were most important:

1. **Scope**

   - Focus on enterprise critical data first; do not attempt to boil the ocean. Govern these at the enterprise level.

   - Lines of business should govern their LOB-critical data, utilizing the tools, processes, standards, and policies developed by the enterprise governance team.

   - Promote an LOB-critical data element to the enterprise critical level, if there is consensus among all trustees and custodians that it belongs in that category.

2. **Education**

   - Educate the senior leadership team on the fact that data governance is an ongoing process and doesn't have an expiration date.

   - Educate employees and board members about the importance of good data governance and the critical role they play in its success.

3. **Communication**

   - Develop a comprehensive communication plan to share status updates, educate, share compliance metrics, share lessons learned, and compare best practices and case studies. Regular communication targeted toward all levels of the organization is critical to the success of the program.

- Schedule brown bags, program deep dives, and hold informational sessions multiple times during the year to communicate the message.

- Invite industry experts to share their successes and to emphasize the value of good governance with key stakeholders.

4. Staffing

- Within each line of business and support function, identify and assign trustees, custodians, and stewards. These resources should be passionate and knowledgeable about data and must be assigned clear roles, responsibilities, authority, and accountability.

- The enterprise governance team must have a clear line of communication to these resources and must collaborate with them to ensure compliance and address systemic data issues.

5. Governance Bodies

- Define a local governance council composed of director- and manager-level staff representing business, operations, and technology departments from each line of business.

- Define a corporate governance council comprised of senior level (officers) staff from business, operations, and technology departments that will address enterprise-level issues and those that are escalated by the local governance council.

6. Change Management

- A key component of any governance program is inculcating behavioral change within every staff member with respect to the stewardship of data.

- Change management is a critical component of this program and must be utilized to affect change across all lines of business and support functions.

7. Culture

- Emphasize continuous improvement of data definitions, data quality, and governance processes, throughout the company.

- Highlight the importance of treating data as a strategic corporate asset by every employee in the company.

- Incorporate data stewardship into the DNA of the organization through awareness, education, and compliance activities.

8. Roles and Responsibilities

- Business departments should be assigned the data trustee and data steward roles and must have clearly defined responsibilities and be empowered to make decisions related to data management.

- Technology and operations teams play a critical advisory role, and support infrastructure, systems, and implementation to sustain the program over the long term. Data custodians typically belong to these teams.

9. Deployment Model

- Use a federated data governance model. Top-down and bottom-up approaches to data governance do not work very well, especially in medium and large sized enterprises.

10. Policies and Standards

- Document and publish corporate-wide data management policies and standards.

- Align them to industry standards (if those standards are mature and have a high level of adoption). This will enable easier integration with business partners and facilitate standardized reporting.

11. Accountability

- Use a carrot-and-stick approach to ensure compliance of LOBs to corporate policies and standards. Tie compliance to staff performance reviews and reward staff members who display the desired behaviors. Educate and take corrective action against those who don't.

- Hold data trustees, data stewards, and data custodians accountable for their organization's compliance to enterprise policies and standards.

12. Procedures

- Define procedures and repeatable processes for identifying and addressing data issues and an escalation process for those issues that cannot be resolved within the first-tier governance council.

13. Metrics

- Capture key performance indicators and key value indicators for the program. Some examples are: compliance to standards, data quality measures by entity and attribute, number of critical data being monitored, number of active rules, adoption of data quality tools and processes, data governance maturity of each LOB, open issues, aging of open issues, and so forth.

* Publish the KPIs, KVIs, and salient metrics monthly to show progress and highlight key accomplishments.

14. Tools and Automation

* Evaluate and select tools for data quality, metadata management, data policy and standards compliance monitoring, and data issue management if there are none available within the enterprise. Tool selection should be based on the enterprise use cases and specific requirements.

* Utilize the data quality tool to automate proactive monitoring of data quality and to remediate any issues.

* Utilize a metadata management tool to capture metadata related to business critical data, data quality rules, business processes, data stores, systems of record, trusted data sources, data lineage, and so forth. Use scanners to scan automatically the metadata sources for updates. Note that some manual intervention may be required to "stitch" metadata.

* Utilize a compliance monitoring tool to automate compliance checks and reporting.

* The enterprise and LOB data management teams should utilize the same set of tools to facilitate compliance with policies and standards and for consistent enterprise and LOB-level reporting.

Conclusion

A paradigm shift is occurring with respect to organizational structure, accountability management, metrics management, and execution strategies is required to address the best practices listed above. Executing against such a paradigm is extremely challenging due to constraints related to legacy systems, immature data management capabilities, siloed business models, siloed data management practices, lack of work flow between components of the information supply chain, internal politics, and market pressures. The right people, processes, and technology and a robust change management program are required to overcome the challenges.

Deploying and sustaining an enterprise-level data governance program can be accomplished, provided it is given the priority it deserves and has the backing of and active participation from senior and line-level managers across business, technology, and operations organizations. There are proven enterprise data governance (EDG) and holistic data quality management (HDQ) frameworks, processes, methodologies, design patterns, and disruptive technical solutions that can be applied to address the data g challenges discussed in this book. It is imperative that corporations invest in them, to improve their regulatory compliance and risk management functions and the overall health of their business-critical data. These are strategic programs that require sponsorship, investment, and ongoing political support from the board and C-level executives. The return on investment is significant, if the program is implemented in a systematic manner, with the proper change management processes and incentives built-in.

Chapter 22

Data Without Context Is Data Porn

Before your mind leaps off the deep end and starts conjuring up images from XXX movies, I should clarify that this chapter is G-rated. In fact, you should encourage your boss and your colleagues to read this chapter, since it will help your career and theirs.

While conducting research, a blog by Brad Feld[1], titled "Three Magic Numbers," caught my attention. In his post, Brad described a visit to a small company that had flat-screen TVs hanging from the ceiling, showing an array of graphs. His mouth was open as he tried to process the data and make sense of it. He knew this particular company well, and could reduce the number of different data points to a small set, but he was completely overwhelmed by the visual display. As he systematically looked at each of the graphs, he realized very few of them mattered much, nor were they particularly helpful in understanding what was going on in the business.

Brad continues: "At the moment I realized these were no longer magic numbers. Instead, I was looking at wallpaper - 'Data Porn.' The entrepreneurial Aeron chair equivalent of 2012. Pretty, but a bad allocation of resources. The 30 people in the room might be looking at the graphs. They might be looking at one of the graphs. But they probably weren't seeing anything."

I'm sure you've encountered similar situations. You were presented with a report or a set of pretty visualizations, but they didn't tell a story, primarily because the data and information presented lacked context.

We are living in the Age of Context[2], since we are bombarded by massive globs of data and need context to make sense of it. The massive globs of big data really don't do anything for the consumer without contextual information. They are *Data Porn*.

I hope I've made my point, connected some dots for you, and given you something to chew on. Next time you are presented with *Data Porn,* demand that the data producer provide context as well. And if you are on the other end, and are spewing massive globs of data, know that you should provide not just data and pretty pictures but the context as well.

Don't get caught producing *Data Porn,* since the morality police will certainly apprehend you and throw you behind bars, putting an end to your illustrious career.

Chapter 23

What's This Thing Called Metadata?

Metadata is probably the most important concept in data management. But it is also the most misunderstood concept and therefore not given the importance it deserves.

Metadata is a rather confusing and technical term, so I prefer to call it "contextual data." I believe contextual data provides a much simpler and clearer meaning and is easier to understand. So, going forward, I will use these terms interchangeably.

You've probably heard the term *metadata* in the context of the National Security Agency's (NSA) collection of metadata on our phone calls (see "We Kill People Based on Metadata"[1]).

Here's what this means in a layperson's terms for the NSA phone call case (courtesy CNN Money, "So What Is Metadata Anyway?"[2]).

- It's information wireless carriers collect about where, when, and to whom customers make phone calls. It doesn't include any recordings of the actual phone calls themselves.

- The metadata can contain phone numbers, the time and duration of calls, and the location of the caller and the recipient.

- It can include which cellular towers were used to transmit the call and what kind of phone was being used.

- When bundled together, those metadata can potentially reveal a whole lot about a caller.

Ex-NSA chief William Hayden states that "Information collected by the NSA about phone calls and other communications that does not include content—can tell the government 'everything' about anyone it's targeting for surveillance, often making the actual content of the communication unnecessary."

This chapter is not about raking up mud about the NSA's program, but presented to show you what metadata is and why it is so important. Organizations can learn from the NSA example and start using metadata to gain a lot more insight into specific subject areas they are interested in—customers, vendors, products, and so forth.

To make this even clearer, let me elaborate a little and provide an example. Different types of contextual data, such as business metadata, operational metadata, process metadata, and technical metadata, can be captured about specific data elements or events. The figure below provides a graphical representation of the different types of metadata that can be captured as data is routed via an extract, transform, and load process.

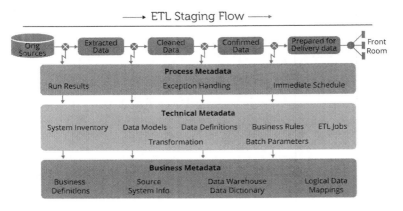

Figure 23.1 Different Types of Metadata *(courtesy E-University)*

Business metadata is typically captured in data dictionaries and glossaries, technical metadata is captured within data modelling tools, database management systems and extract, transform, and load (ETL) tools, and process metadata is captured in various other systems. All this contextual information is very beneficial to programmers, database developers, analysts, and data scientists in their daily tasks.

Some other important aspects of contextual data are:

- Contextual data is critical for processing big data, since Hadoop is based on a "Schema on Read" paradigm and therefore has no contextual information about the data on read.

- Contextual data is required to better define data quality requirements.

- Contextual data helps in data discovery and search functions, something that most business and data analysts and data scientists do as part of their data discovery and analysis work. The purpose of all this metadata is to drive discoverability and increase sales.

- Contextual data is used to annotate reports and in analytics.

- Contextual data can also inform data consumers of the data about who is accountable for it from a governance perspective, which business processes use it, and which data domain it belongs to.

- Contextual data should be a critical component of every organization's data management program.

Establishing a metadata repository[3], seeding it with contextual data, and maintaining the data over time will provide significant benefits. There are metadata management tools in the marketplace that can be utilized, or firms can start with simple Microsoft Excel–based templates and then graduate to a commercial system.

Chapter 24

Real World Data Quality

I n the chapter titled *Data Quality is Job 1 and Here's Why?,* I made the case that every organization should introduce the slogan "Data Quality is Job 1" so that data quality gets woven into its DNA. In this chapter, I will help you understand this complex topic and connect the dots on the impact that poor data quality has on your organization, from cost, decision-making, and operations perspectives. Data quality is also gaining attention because it is impacting the time-to-value of big data and IOT projects.

I led the enterprise data quality organization at a Fortune 10 firm and built the program from the ground up. This assignment gave me the opportunity to study the intimate details of data quality, understand its impact on the organization, roll out a data quality architecture and benchmarking capability, develop strategies that would benefit individual departments and the enterprise, and develop training material to educate and raise awareness across thousands of employees across eight divisions. I also had to influence senior management to gain sponsorship to weave data quality into the culture.

"We know that data scientists are valuable for their companies, but there's still a disconnect between what they actually do and what they want to do," Lukas Biewald, cofounder and CEO of CrowdFlower[1], said in a statement.

"At the end of the day, the time they invest in cleaning data is time that could be better spent doing strategic, creative work like predictive analysis or data mining. If companies can give data scientists some of that data cleaning time back, they'll have happier teams that can focus on really exciting things."

My firm has been involved in several data projects. Our experience shows that teams typically spend 60 to 70 percent of their time preparing data for analysis. Data cleansing activities consume a significant portion of that.

Let me pause here and give you an opportunity to think about this. Please write down your definition of data quality and indicate how you would measure it. This is an important step and something that I'd like you to do, since it will give you an opportunity to compare your definition and measurement criteria with mine, after you've read this chapter.

Data quality is a nebulous term, and each of us has a different definition for it. Here's one that is most often cited in data management literature:

"There are many definitions of data quality but data is generally considered high quality if, 'they are fit for their intended uses in operations, decision-making and planning." - J. M. Juran[2]

The key words here are "fit for intended uses." This implies that the data consumer decides the data quality requirements based on the intended uses of that data. This is a slippery slope, since it makes it very difficult for us to create a single set of data quality requirements for a particular data element (e.g., loan ID) or dataset, and it is compounded by the fact that, in most instances, there may be multiple definitions of a particular data element. The "fit for intended uses" dimension is one aspect of data quality, but there are other dimensions that have to be considered as well. I will describe these below.

Many firms have dozens of definitions for a single data element, and it is impossible to gain consensus on a single one. Which definition does one use when defining the data quality requirements? Let me throw another variable into the mix—*a temporal aspect. Data can change states and the data quality requirements can be different for each state* (e.g., a loan can start in the origination state, change to the underwriting state, and then move into the delivered state, and the quality requirements are different for each state—depending on specific policies, products, and exceptions under consideration).

Let me add another wrinkle to this. *Data quality requirements are tied to policies, and policies tend to change over time.* For example, there could be a policy today that requires certain data elements, such as race and income, to be mandatory on a delivered loan, but this policy could change in the future to make the data elements optional. *This policy change has a direct impact on the data quality checks that have to be performed.* If you weren't aware of such policy changes and looked at historical data in isolation, you might conclude that the data had quality issues (i.e., it has missing or incomplete data), but in reality this isn't the case.

I'd like to share a real-life story to make this tangible, since I dealt with all of the above issues at a firm that got its investor disclosures wrong. The CEO of this heavily regulated Fortune 500 firm received a call from the head of a very large institutional investor the day after the new disclosures were published. The CEO was informed that the PhD quants at the investor's firm had analyzed the disclosures and concluded that they were incorrect and had significant quality issues. These disclosures were used to make multimillion dollar investment decisions. Poor quality disclosures could potentially cause significant financial impact and posed serious risk for the institutional investor. This wasn't desirable for all parties.

Imagine the CEO's reaction, since this incident risked the firm's reputation and had significant legal and financial implications. He had been told by the project team that they had conducted months of testing to ensure that the disclosures were correct. To make a long story short, his firm had to hire an army of high-paid consultants, pull a majority of the operations staff, and run a round-the-clock operation to get to the bottom of it. After several months and several million dollars of expenses, the team concluded that the primary reasons for this issue were: (1) incorrect assumptions made by the disclosures team about the systems of record for specific data elements, (2) while data wasn't incorrect or missing, policy changes that occurred in the past had caused certain data elements to be blank, and this should have been reported to the investors, and (3) rigorous data quality checks were applied only to a subset of the disclosed data rather than the entire set, because the officer in charge of the project felt it was too expensive. ***The moral of this story is simple: It pays to invest in data quality.***

By now, you are probably beginning to realize why this is such a complex topic and why most of us struggle with it. It is much easier to define the quality requirements and specifications for a mechanical component that is being fabricated and measure its quality than it is to define the quality of a data element. For data, a lot more contextual information and understanding of the specific use of any given data is required, before you can clearly articulate the quality requirements and measurement criteria.

A summary of the highlights follows:

- Data quality is a very complex topic.

- One has to understand the definition and context related to a specific data element or set of data before defining data quality requirements.

- Data changes states and is impacted by policy changes. The data quality requirements have to take these issues into consideration.

- Data quality requirements are primarily driven by the data's intended use.

Therefore, the data consumer is ultimately responsible for, and is the right person(s) to define, the data quality requirements and the data quality measurement criteria (e.g., quality thresholds, targets, and dimensions).

I have tried to demystify data quality for you and help you connect the dots. "Fit for intended uses" is one dimension of data quality, but there are other dimensions that must be considered as well—definition and context, temporal aspects, and policy implications. Please think about this topic, take one or two data elements that you work with, and apply the concepts I've discussed above. Share the lessons learned and key observations with your team and use them to develop a data quality framework, measurement criteria and data profiling capabilities.

Chapter 25

What's This Thing Called RDM?

RDM is closely related to and is a prerequisite for successfully implementing master data management (MDM). In fact, companies implementing MDM are forced to address RDM to ensure that they are able to get the master data records right. For details on MDM, please refer to the chapter titled *What's This Thing Called MDM?*.

Let me share a couple of examples of RDM to make things easier for you. Reference data is a set of valid values for a particular data field, and it typically applies to data fields that are commonly used across an organization. Reference data is also used to decode data. For example, a data provider may send you a product code, which you would have to decode in order to report on it.

Most companies manage customer addresses, and city, state, and zip code are typically mandatory fields of the address record. In order to validate these field applications, check them against reference data sets of cities, states, and zip codes provided by the US Postal Service. The same goes for product categories, gender types, or any other field that needs to be validated against a reference data set.

Some companies have implemented RDM and are able to provide a single set of reference data for various data fields, but many of them haven't. Companies that don't have RDM in place end up maintaining the codes in silos, increasing the likelihood of miscoding items and adding significant overhead during the extract, transform, and load processing steps. Not having a single set of reference data also impacts reporting and analytics.

Why is RDM important? It is important because it enables organizations to create a standard set of allowable values that can be used across all applications, promotes standard coding and decoding practices, results in good quality data, and eliminates the management and reconciliation effort required to handle multiple copies of reference data.

There are several off-the-shelf commercial products that enable organizations to capture, manage, and deploy reference data.

Chapter 26

What's This Thing Called MDM?

MDM stands for master data management and represents a single point of reference for important data such as customers, employees, products, vendors, accounts, and so forth.

Customer data, for example, may be collected via multiple channels: front-end applications, such as order entry or reservations, and offline transactions, such as surveys or via other electronic means. This data has to be validated, matched, and merged with existing customer data to ensure that duplicates aren't being generated and enriched with additional data.

Without an MDM solution in place, the data validation, match and merge, and enrichment logic isn't centralized or standardized across business processes, resulting in data fragmentation and inconsistencies. This creates serious impacts for businesses: an inability to gain a 360-degree view of a customer, an inability to get a single master record of a customer, an inability to determine all transactions conducted by a customer; and so forth. Sales and marketing, revenue management, finance, planning and accounting, corporate systems, product management, and human resources are some of the organizations that are impacted by a lack of master data.

As a data practitioner, it is easy for me to identify companies that do not have an MDM solution in place when I receive multiple offers from them for the same promotion, as they contain different names and slightly different addresses, or I get bombarded by e-mails for various offerings.

Let me share an example to make things clearer. I signed up for an online investment advisory service recently and decided to cancel it after a week. The vendor acknowledged my cancellation via e-mail, but continued to bombard me with other e-mails related to various offerings. I opened a couple of the e-mails and clicked on the "Unsubscribe" button, hoping that this would take care of the problem. It didn't. I continued to receive multiple e-mails a day from them. The conclusion I can draw from this is that their ordering, sales, and marketing systems aren't synchronized with their campaign management systems, an MDM-related problem.

I am sure you've encountered such situations as well and can relate to my predicament. It's certainly frustrating for the customer, but imagine the expense side of the equation for vendors, since they are incurring mailing costs, processing costs, and costs for maintaining numerous copies of the same data across data stores. The inability to have a single reference dataset also impacts vendors' ability to analyze customer data holistically in order to gain insights such as value of the customer, the customer's shopping behavior, the customer's social profile, and so forth, which directly impacts their bottom line (i.e., cross-sell/up-sell, product innovation, personalization, or targeted promotions).

Chapter 27

What's This Thing Called Big Data?

Big data[1] is a buzzword that's been floating around for the last few years and has gained some mind-share among the masses. In my advisory role, I tend to be asked this question regularly, especially by business leaders. They typically receive unsolicited e-mails regarding big data offerings or attend online webinars on big data or happen to be at a conference where big data is discussed in the context of marketing, product management, customer engagement, and so forth.

Big is a relative term and mainframes and supercomputers have been crunching massive amounts of data for years. So why the sudden craze for big data? Why did someone have to invent the term big data and spin up a whole industry around it? Let me share some historical context with you, since that will help you understand the drivers for building out this whole new framework for processing large amounts of data.

Google and Yahoo! played a key role in developing the Hadoop[2] framework, which is used in processing big data. In order to support their business models, they needed the following capabilities (which were lacking in the traditional relational database management systems):

- Ability to process massive amounts of semi-structured and unstructured data generated at a high velocity due to the online activities of their users.

- Ability to scale horizontally, by adding more computing power (nodes) rather than having to constantly expand memory and CPUs in existing servers.

+ Ability to define the structure and relationships between the data at the time of processing (schema on read) rather than at the time of storage (schema on write).

+ Ability to self-heal. They were "always-on" enterprises and needed a self-healing capability, which could deal with hardware failures gracefully and not impact processing.

You've probably read or heard about the "3 V's of big data,"[3] volume, velocity, and variety that was introduced to us by Gartner (then Meta Group) analyst Doug Laney in the late 1990's. I'm not going to delve into them here, since you can find many articles on the V's if you Google the term.

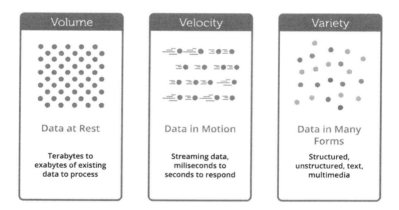

Figure 27.1 The 3 V's of Big Data

What I am going to share with you are some of the reasons why the Hadoop framework, which is used to process big data, was created:

+ It is self-healing.

+ It scales horizontally, by adding more nodes, as needed.

- It runs on commodity hardware.

- It supports cloud computing.,

- It doesn't need a predefined schema at the time of persistence, but schema can be generated on read or when one processes the data.

- It is able to process unstructured and semi-structured data.

In closing, big data refers to a capability that enables organizations to process very large amounts of data in a cost-effective manner. This capability is being utilized by organizations to gain deeper insights, get answers to complex questions, run predictive analytics, utilize machine learning, and leverage other capabilities to drive sales, marketing, planning, R&D, and so on.

Vendors such as MapR, Hortonworks, and Cloudera offer Hadoop distributions to give organizations the ability to harness the power of big data. Data analytics vendors such as Tableau, Qlik, Spotfire, Birst, Microstrategy, SAS, Alteryx, ZoomData, Databricks, and Datameer provide the advanced visualization capability that organizations need. Several data wrangling tools such as Trifacta have gained prominence recently due to their ability to automate the data preparation and data understanding steps in the analytics journey. Products such as Waterline Data Inventory automate finding, understanding, and governing data in Hadoop. Alation provides the capability for companies to centralize data knowledge and how best to use it, unlocking the unrealized insights in both their data systems and their most-experienced employees. Informatica, IBM, and SAS provide a suite of products for managing, integrating data and analyzing it.

Building a big data platform requires investment, specialized skills, and a strong business case, and it may not be for every organization. Implementing a big data platform also requires a certain amount of data management and governance maturity.

Disclaimer: This is not an exhaustive list, but a sample. The inclusion of a vendor in this chapter shouldn't be construed as a recommendation or endorsement on my part. An organization wishing to select big data technology, data governance, and analytics product(s) should undertake thorough market research and conduct a formal evaluation, based on its specific requirements.

Chapter 28

What's This Thing Called IOT?

ontinuing with the "What's This Thing?" theme, let's discuss IOT[1] in this chapter, a topic that is gaining momentum in the marketplace, especially as wearable and sensor devices become ubiquitous.

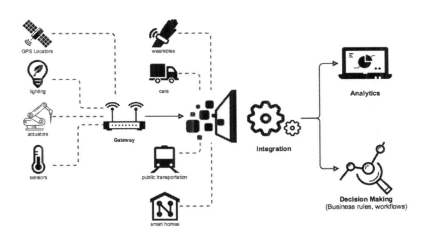

Figure 28.1 The Internet of Things Architecture
(Štefan Bunčiak)

New devices or things such as wearables are being embedded within technology, giving them the ability to instantaneously send and receive data over the Internet without human or computer intervention. This sensor capability is available in numerous other devices that we use: automobiles, refrigerators, garage doors, lights, thermostats, and so on, and more devices are going to be offered with these capabilities in the future. These things are connected to, and communicate via, the Internet and therefore can be controlled remotely, can share data with other devices in real time, and have some level of intelligence built-in.

Organizations that capture and process IOT-generated data can gain deeper insights into the operating status of the device, the behavior of the user, or the sequence of events that have occurred in order to troubleshoot issues. IOT data can be combined with location data to gain even more insights.

IOT provides opportunities for product innovation, service improvement, and deeper insights into customer behavior across all verticals, especially in the healthcare, financial services, hospitality, and retail domains.

PART EIGHT

Take Steps to Win with Data

Chapter 29

Use the Data Management Maturity Model to Develop a Roadmap for Success

Before embarking on a journey, one needs a roadmap, a navigation system, and an acute awareness of the surroundings. External events such as bad weather, accidents, construction work, and system emergencies require adjustment to the route. This is true of organizations that are embarking on building out an enterprise data management, governance, and analytics program or considering adjustments to an existing program that isn't delivering the expected value.

The first step in the journey should be to conduct a data management maturity assessment.[1] It will highlight the strengths and weaknesses of an organization's maturity, identify areas for improvement, and potentially be used as a guide while developing a roadmap for achieving the desired level of maturity and sophistication.

The Software Engineering Institute at Carnegie Mellon University[2] developed the Data Management Maturity Model (DMM), which defines five levels of maturity, starting at a highly immature and reactive level (Level 1) and extending to a highly mature, automated, and optimized level (Level 5). Since you can't improve what you can't measure, the DMM provides a standard mechanism to measure the maturity of an organization's data management people, process, and technology capabilities.

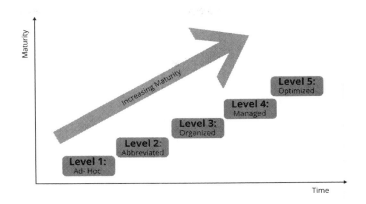

Figure 29.1 Capability Maturity Levels

The DMM measures the maturity across five categories: (1) data management strategy, (2) data governance, (3) data quality, (4) platform and architecture, and (5) data operations. Additional details are available at http://cmmiinstitute.com/data-management-maturity.

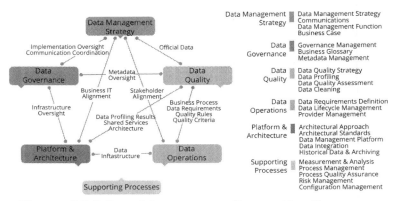

Figure 29.2 Data Management Supporting Processes

In addition to the other categories, organizations can use the DMM for data quality, to determine their level of data quality maturity. It can also be used to develop a data quality roadmap to mature their people, processes, and technology, and reach the desired level of maturity.

I have participated in several data management maturity assessments over the years and find that they provide useful information about the organization's leadership team, help make a case for investing in data quality management, and show the benefits that can be achieved as a result.

Many firms provide data quality maturity assessments as a service or as a component of a larger data management maturity assessment. This is usually accomplished via a series of meetings with key stakeholders from the data, business, technology, and operations teams to discuss various topics related to data and to gather anecdotes and real-life examples that are indicative of the organization's maturity, followed by a set of questionnaires and surveys to key personnel to capture metrics related to maturity. All these data points are then used and plotted in a spider diagram, which provides a visual representation of the maturity level across various dimensions.

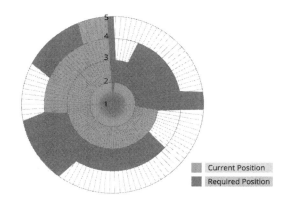

Figure 29.3 Maturity Level across Dimensions

In the diagram above, the light-yellow areas could represent the current DMM maturity of an organization across the five DMM categories discussed above, and the lavender areas could represent the required DMM maturity, based on an organization's specific needs. Such a diagram can be used to start charting out a roadmap to get to the desired DMM level.

Chapter 30

The Organizational Culture Change Journey

> *"Culture does not change because we desire to change it. Culture changes when the organization is transformed; the culture reflects the realities of people working together every day." – Mark Sanborn*

I hope you are convinced by now, that data is a strategic asset, and needs a seat at the table. It's not the data that's important, but our ability to generate interesting insight from it that matters the most. A data culture is an essential prerequisite to winning in a highly competitive environment.

There are two key areas worth exploring at this stage (1) how does one define culture, and (2) what's the most effective way to change an organization's culture to implement a data culture.

Defining Culture

Culture and organizational change are very complex topics. I am not an expert in both these fields but have participated in several change initiatives over the last two decades. In order to educate myself about these topics, and understand how leaders have successfully implemented change, I researched these topics and the key findings are presented below.

While conducting research, I chanced upon an interesting article titled *What is Organizational Culture Change? And Why Should We Care?*[1] It provided the information I was looking for, regarding the topics of culture, and organizational change. The article discussed the fact that while there is universal agreement that (1) culture exists, and (2) that culture plays a crucial role in shaping behavior in organizations, there is little consensus on what organizational culture actually is, never mind how it influences behavior and whether it is something leaders can change.

The authors continue by quoting Aristotle - "We are what we repeatedly do". According to them, this view elevates repeated behavior or habits as the core of culture and deemphasizes what people feel, think or believe. It also focuses our attention on the forces that shape behavior in organizations, and so highlights an important question: are all those forces (including structure, processes, and incentives) "culture" or is culture simply the behavioral outputs?

It continues with the following assertion: "cultures of organizations are never monolithic. There are many factors that drive internal variations in the culture of business functions (e.g. finance vs. marketing) and units (e.g. a fast-moving consumer products division vs. a pharmaceuticals division of a diversified firm). A company's history of acquisition also figures importantly in defining its culture and sub-cultures. Depending on how acquisition and integration are managed, the legacy cultures of acquired units can persist for surprisingly long periods of time."

Implementing Organizational Culture Change

How does an organization transform itself to incorporate a data culture? There are two schools of thought regarding the best method for culture change (1) transform organizations by introducing new changes to "fix" the culture, or (2) consider culture change as something you get after you've put new processes, and structures in place, to tackle complex business problems.

In a Harvard Business Review (HBR) article titled *Culture is not the Culprit,*[2] the authors conclude that culture change isn't something you "fix", but rather culture change is what you get after you've put new processes or structure in place, to tackle complex business problems, and that culture evolves as important work is done. This conclusion is based on interviews with several current and former CEOs who have successfully led major transformations.

The leaders the authors spoke with took different approaches for different ends, and the article provides some examples. Alan Mulally worked to break down barriers between units at Ford, whereas Dan Vasella did a fair amount of decentralizing to unleash creative energy at Novartis. But in every case, when the leaders used tools such as decision rights, performance measurement, and reward systems to address their particular business challenges, organizational culture evolved in interesting ways as a result, reinforcing the new direction.

In the wake of the General Motors (GE) recall issues, CEO Mary Barra introduced new edicts to "create the right environment" – by improving accountability across the firm to "fix" its culture. She's had mixed results.

The HBR article describes several examples of culture change introduced by the leadership – to deal with post-merger and acquisition integration challenges (e.g., Ecolab), gaining employee trust to drive growth (e.g., Delta's acquisition of Northwest Airlines in 2008), turning around a company that was close to bankruptcy post-financial crash of 2008 (e.g., Ford Motor Company), and post-merger challenges (e.g., merger of Sandoz and Ciba-Geigy). In all instances, the CEO's started with a clear sense of purpose and then went about introducing changes to achieve it. They used various methods such as introducing new incentive schemes, breaking down barriers between departments by forcing interaction and transparency, and providing training to front line staff to improve customer service.

Chip Heath[3] is currently a professor of organizational behavior at Stanford University and has written extensively on the topic of organizational change. In his book titled "Switch: How to Change Things When Change Is Hard,"[4] he explains that change stalls if it is not influenced through analytical and emotional sides. The rational side understands that the company needs to change, but the emotional side is comfortable with the old ways of thinking and is skeptical about the company changing successfully.

Leaders have a tendency to focus on the analytical, and not on the emotional drivers, he states. Senior leaders can play a critical role in influencing change, by creating a positive environment, and making the journey easier for their associates. They should use the core strengths of the organization, and what it has done well in the past, as the impetus for change.

Chip states that lots of research in behavioral economics shows that too much choice is paralyzing. Especially within a change situation, a big part of freeing up the creativity needed for change may be simplifying internal processes.

The Change Journey

In order to successfully implement change within an organization, leaders will require a roadmap and an execution strategy.

Here's what a change journey may look like –

- Acknowledge at the board and CEO level that a data culture is required, to succeed with data.

- Assess current culture, identify strengths and weaknesses, and areas that must be addressed to become a data culture.

- Develop a business case for change, based on specific benefits to the organization – using analytical and emotional rationale. Align the culture change initiative to a larger business initiative such as improving customer service, diversifying product offering, or improving financials (similar to what the leaders at Ecolab, Ford, Novartis and Delta did).

- Develop a change management plan, with clear objectives, critical success factors (CSF), training plan, and a roadmap.

- Develop a communication plan, and clearly document and communicate the habits that will and won't be tolerated. Reward those that display the desired habits, through monetary rewards or by promoting them.

- Get the senior management team on board (i.e., leader-of-leaders), and then trickle this down to every level of the organization.

- Educate and train senior management in core SDM and data science concepts, and specific methodologies such as agile and lean. This should be followed by customized training for associates, based on their individual role and responsibilities.

- Measure progress against CSFs and communicate regularly across the organization, highlighting what's working, what's not and making the necessary adjustments.

Change programs will certainly encounter roadblocks. Adequate time and resources should be allocated to for overcoming them, during the execution phase.

I believe every member of an organization is a leader, and should act as one. Some are lucky enough to move up the ranks, and become leaders of leaders. They are assigned impressive titles, and held to a higher level of responsibility and expected to lead by example. Regardless of their title, every associate plays a critical role in the success of his or her department's change initiative.

The five key takeaways for leaders are (1) clearly articulate why the change is being introduced (i.e., its purpose) and what the tangible benefits of the change would be, (2) create an emotional case for change, not just an analytical one, and tie it to customers, products, or employees, (3) highlight organizational strengths, and recent or past successes, and take them into consideration while developing the execution strategy for the change initiative, (4) use their position of power within the organization to guide the change, and (5) provide the necessary air cover to remove impediments.

In order to succeed in their change journey, leaders can take inspiration from Apple's revolutionary "Think Different"[5] advertisement campaign, and "To the Crazy Ones" commercial. This was the commercial that played a pivotal role in helping Apple achieve one of the greatest corporate turnarounds in business history.

"Here's to the crazy ones. The misfits. The rebels. The troublemakers. The round pegs in the square holes. The ones who see things differently. They're not fond of rules. And they have no respect for the status quo. You can quote them, disagree with them, glorify or vilify them. About the only thing you can't do is ignore them. Because they change things. They push the human race forward. And while some may see them as the crazy ones, we see genius. Because the people who are crazy enough to think they can change the world, are the ones who do."
—*Rob Siltanen*

Below are some key passages from the movie *Dead Poets Society* that served as inspiration for the Apple script.

"We must constantly look at things in a different way. Just when you think you know something, you must look at it in a different way. Even though it may seem silly or wrong, you must try. Dare to strike out and find new ground."

"Despite what anyone might tell you, words and ideas can change the world."

"We don't read and write poetry because it's cute. We read and write poetry because we are members of the human race. And the human race is filled with passion. Poetry, beauty, love, romance. These are what we stay alive for. The powerful play goes on and you may contribute a verse. What will your verse be?"

Chapter 31

Ten Guiding Principles

I n order to bring about change, leaders should set some guiding principles to act as a framework for their organizations. I'd like to share ten that you may wish to consider:

1. **The "Golden Square" rules:** People, Process, Technology, and Data dimensions must be incorporated into all programs, and become a part of the operating language.

2. **Simplicity wins:** Small and big data ecosystems are very complex. Organizations have to simplify things and adopt a *"Keep It Simple"* rule to succeed. Every individual must focus on keeping things as simple as possible – data models, data architecture, data processing, and physical data stores.

3. **Be transparent:** As compliance mandates become stringent, organizations will be required to maintain *data management process transparency.* It's a good practice to incorporate process transparency as a standard operating practice within your organization.

4. **Data quality is key:** Don't compromise on that by taking shortcuts.

5. **Secure sensitive data:** Protect sensitive data by preventing unauthorized access, and using all means at your disposal, to prevent it from getting into the wrong hands.

6. **Context is king:** In this "Age of Data" capture context related to all aspects of the business (i.e., transactions, processes, transformations, analytics models, data etc.), ideally in a central repository, and strive to keep it current

7. **Continuously mature people, process and technology:** Organizations that wish to win with data, must invest in continuously maturing their people, process, and technology.

8. **Create a learning environment:** Capture knowledge from across the enterprise centrally and democratize it, to enable a learning environment.

9. **Do the right thing and do things right:** Taking shortcuts and being too tactical most of the time, results in serious consequences for the organization.

10. **Trust but verify:** Never blindly trust the numbers you are presented with. Learn to ask the right questions about the provenance, lineage, the system(s) of truth, and challenge the authenticity and quality of the underlying data.

Conclusion

For too long, data has been considered a byproduct of business transactions and taken for granted, but not given the importance it deserves. This must change. Organizations that wish to succeed with data must transform themselves and incorporate a data culture. *They must pivot around data rather than IT!*

In an article published in January 2016[1], Klaus Schwab, the founder and executive chairman of the World Economic Forum stated, "We stand on the brink of a technological revolution that will fundamentally alter the way we live, work, and relate to one another. In its scale, scope, and complexity, the transformation will be unlike anything humankind has experienced before. We do not yet know just how it will unfold, but one thing is clear: the response to it must be integrated and comprehensive, involving all stakeholders of the global polity, from the public and private sectors to academia and civil society."

Klaus continues that the First Industrial Revolution used water and steam power to mechanize production. The Second used electric power to create mass production. The Third used electronics and information technology to automate production. *Now a Fourth Industrial Revolution is building on the Third, the digital revolution that has been occurring since the middle of the last century. It is characterized by a fusion of technologies that is blurring the lines between the physical, digital, and biological spheres. In order to make this point, I've labeled the Fourth Industrial Revolution the "Age of Data."*

Organizations and their leaders are at a crossroad – intersection of tumultuous market changes and the opportunities presented by the world of big data and IOT. Will they embrace change and unleash the power of their data assets to propel their organizations forward and achieve their MISSION or get disrupted? The answer lies in their willingness to embrace data as their friend and to stand up for data. This can only be done if there is true understanding of data, the context within which it exists and is used, understanding of the data management vocabulary, and the ability to ask the right questions when presented with a set of numbers, reports, or the output of analytical models.

In a nutshell, the leaders of tomorrow will be data-driven since the new leadership model requires it as a core skill. Data-driven leaders will in turn drive a data culture through a change agenda, lead by example, and train their associates in the latest data management methodologies, tools and techniques.

The world of data is complex and will continue to become more complex as new constructs are formulated (e.g., Blockchain and Bitcoin), new data processing frameworks evolve (Hadoop and post Hadoop) and the associated technology matures. During this time of massive change, leaders have to not just "keep the trains running," but strategically position their organizations to take advantage of their data assets and execute against a vision of "competing with data". Their success will be tied to their ability to be change agents, their superior ability to strategize and execute on their vision, and their ability to assemble high performing teams.

There are numerous examples of data-driven leaders that have delivered on this vision. The common traits that they possess are - data savvy, appetite for risk taking, interest in technology, innovative and their clarity of vision of what they wanted their firms to do and be. Some examples of such leaders are Larry Page and Sergey Brin (Google), Jeff Bezos (Amazon), Mark Zuckerberg (Facebook), Max Levchin (PayPal), Pierre Omidyar (eBay), Steve Jobs (Apple), Reid Hoffman (LinkedIn), Jack Dorsey (Twitter), and Reed Hastings (Netflix).

Traditional businesses that grew up in the "Brick and Mortar" era are at a significant disadvantage in the "Age of Data." Competition is tough and data-driven companies such as Amazon.com are causing massive disruption across the board - in retail, publication, books, groceries, and electronics. The same is true of state and federal agencies that are experiencing budgetary pressure and are being forced to become more transparent (e.g., open data initiative) and adapt new and agile methods of delivery.

Leaders are faced with many challenges on a day-to-day basis and are forced to make decisions in real time based on limited data. They never have enough time in their schedule, they have to meet aggressive goals, and their tenure at the helm is determined by how well they meet their numbers. In some ways, the C-suite is a revolving door.

According to a March 2015 study by Spencer Stuart[2], the CMO tenure has doubled since 2004 to forty-eight months, and that the longer tenure is primarily a reflection of CMOs' worth and impact on their companies. These savvy veterans have firmly planted themselves at the right hand of the CEO for many years and they have become increasingly valuable assets for some very large companies.

Being a CMO is a complicated task, requiring a diverse set of skills, said Tony Pace, global CMO of Subway FAF and a study participant, who has held his job for seventy-two months. "It takes excellent strategic skills, the ability to translate your marketing strategy into messaging to reach your target audience," he said. "With all of the data out there now, you need good analytical skills." Historically, unlike other roles in the C-suite, "as a CMO, you get one shot then you're pushed out," he said. But CMOs are becoming increasingly invaluable assets. "Anyone can count the beans; not too many can make the beans. In a world that's going more transparent, the skills that you have as CMO are actually better preparation to be a CEO than they've ever been. The top person has got to have the ability to communicate, and you're better prepared for that coming out of the marketing function. If an organization is going to succeed, it's got to grow its customer base, and nobody's better at doing that than the marketing people."

I've broken the data management domain into the following six major tiers, which build upon one another:

1. *Persistence tier:* SQL and NoSQL stores, Hadoop, etc.

2. *Transformation tier:* Transform and load data into the persistence tier

3. *Capability tier:* Data quality, context (i.e., Metadata), data catalog, security, and master and reference data

4. *Knowledge tier:* Combination of crowd sourced and manually entered data to capture institutional knowledge - knowledge related to the business critical data, business processes, and semantics

5. *Process tier:* Governance, authorization, issue management, configuration management, and data integration

6. *Insights tier:* Mine vast quantities of data to gain deep insights. Various industry terms for this are data science, machine learning, artificial intelligence, data mining, analytics, and business intelligence.

Although in some chapters I discuss the "How", my intention was not to delve too deeply into that – but to stay focused on the "Why". I may address the "What" and "How" in a subsequent book, if there is significant demand from readers.

In order to bring their data vision to fruition, organizations need a data strategy, an execution roadmap, and laser-focused execution to leverage the power of data. In this journey, they will have to assemble a team of skilled resources, develop a change agenda, incorporate new technologies and infrastructure into the ecosystem, and focus on world class execution capabilities. Many new capabilities and technologies and changes will be introduced into the organization, which should not disrupt day-to-day operations. That's a tough balancing act and requires precision execution.

By now you've probably realized that it takes a village to properly manage and govern data – if organizations wish to gain deeper insights, make predictions, understand correlations between data and ultimately drive better results. There is also a dark side of data that you must be aware of – quality, security, and privacy being three important dimensions of that dark side. It takes a multifaceted approach to address these areas – a combination of human intelligence, algorithms, proactive monitoring and reactive root-cause analysis, combined with remediation.

As organizations get overwhelmed by the sheer volume and velocity of data, there is an increased tendency to depend purely on algorithms to analyze it and react. However, in the rush to meet aggressive numbers, leaders mustn't lose sight of the human factor. By this I am referring to domain knowledge, intuition, contextual knowledge, data science skills, and common sense, that are required during each stage of the analytical process – business understanding, data understanding, data preparation, modeling, evaluation and deployment.

Data, if used properly can be extremely beneficial, but can cause havoc, if misused. That's another reason for leaders to become data savvy – so that they are aware of the opportunities and challenges that data presents, and arm themselves with enough knowledge about the fields of data management and data science to be able to ask the right questions and make the right evidence-based decisions.

I hope you will take some time out of your busy schedule to reflect upon the topics discussed in this book and the questions that were raised. My intention is that you use the knowledge gained to trigger a debate within your organization

– with respect to its data management and data science maturity and the actions required to build a data culture and innovate with data.

I'd like to close by re-iterating what Dr. Kirk Borne states so eloquently in the foreword –

"Data drives results for at least three major functional requirements in any domain (whether it is business, or science, or government, or education, or whatever): (1) discovery, (2) decision making, and (3) value-creation (i.e., innovation). The best ROI metric (if you can quantify it) would be Return On Innovation through data-driven processes, people, and products.

Data collections are now recognized as a core business asset, a new natural resource, a driver of business change and innovation, a source of increased and/or new revenue streams, a creative force for new products and new markets, and a job opportunity bonanza for those with essential data skills."

APPENDIX

Recap of the Major Themes Discussed

Since we live a significant portion of our lives in the digital world and leave an ever-increasing digital trail, data is being created all the time. Most organizations are seeing their data volumes rise by 30 to 50 percent every year. Private and public sector companies have to manage, govern, and analyze this data to generate insights, manage risk, and create business value. This is a complex undertaking and most organizations are struggling to cope. Nimble rivals, much more sophisticated in technology, big data management, and data science, are either disrupting traditional competitors or threatening to take over a significant portion of their market share.

In this new world order, organizations must continuously innovate and improvise using data to stay relevant. Along with the massive opportunities the data deluge presents, it poses some serious challenges as well. Organizations have to secure sensitive data to ensure its privacy, create golden copies of customer, product, and vendor data (i.e., master data), extract contextual data related to processes and specific data elements, and ensure that the quality of business-critical data is constantly monitored and remediated and that the right level of data governance is in place. This is even more of a business imperative for highly regulated industries such as those in financial services, healthcare, energy and utilities, life sciences, and pharmaceuticals.

Data Deluge

- We are witnessing the *Dawn of Data*. Organizations are capturing and storing massive amounts of data but aren't able to unleash its full potential.

- Private and public sector companies will have to become data-driven in order to derive business value from data and prevent themselves from getting disrupted.

- Since companies and organizations are comprised of people and led by a group of leaders, it is important that all associates and leaders become data literate, data savvy, and data-driven.

- In the new Leadership 2.0 model, leaders and organizations must start using the Golden Square rule and address people, process, technology, and data, not just people, process, and technology.

- Instead of pivoting around IT, leaders must pivot around data.

Dark Data and the Dark Side of Data

- Research shows that organizations possess massive amounts of rich data, but 85 percent of it is not used for any meaningful purpose. This is called Dark Data.

- There is a massive opportunity and revenue cost associated with Dark Data. It should be discovered and unleashed.

- Data must be trustworthy for it to have value to consumers. Unfortunately, high quality isn't readily available in many organizations.

- Publishing and sharing poor quality data results in bad decisions and low quality analytics and impacts the bottom line.

Perils of Not Investing in SDM

- Big data and IOT present opportunities, but they can be hard to implement in traditional organizations that are used to dealing only with structured data and a specific set of use cases.

- Many companies are investing heavily in big data and IOT projects with limited success. Their rate of success can improve dramatically if they follow industry best practices, learn from the experiences of successful big data and IOT implementations, and engage with and get advice from thought leaders and firms that specialize in big data. Finally, they should treat this process as a marathon and not a sprint.

Who's on Point for Data?

- Since data is a strategic asset, it must be treated as such, and there must be senior leadership assigned to drive data management, governance, quality, and analytics.

- "Information is power." So, whoever controls it wields great power within an organization. This can result in the creation of data fiefdoms and data silos and introduces politics.

- Data fiefdoms, data silos, and the politics associated with them can have serious consequences for organizations if left unaddressed. An organization can't become data-driven and extract maximum business value from its data unless it can liberate data and create a culture of shared ownership of data.

Data Management Challenges

- Senior leaders and data consumers need high quality data and information in the right format at the right time. However, within many organizations, those needs aren't being fulfilled.

- There are four primary reasons for this: (1) lack of an organization-wide data catalog, (2) lack of accountability for data (e.g., weak governance), (3) missing contextual information, and (4) lack of organization-wide quality standards, policies, and implementations.

- There is a major disconnect between business and IT departments in many organizations. In many cases, the relationship is so bad that it borders on being dysfunctional. This has serious ramifications for the organization's mission, and it must be addressed.

Building a Data-Driven Company

- Research has shown that companies that are data-driven are more successful than their peers are.

- Investing in SDM creates an opportunity for organizations to diversify their revenue streams by monetizing data—by creating data products or selling enriched datasets.

- It is possible to create a multibillion-dollar business or a line of business within an organization by monetizing data and analytics.

- The six key ingredients for a successful data-driven organization are: (1) foster a startup culture, (2) always focus on customers' needs, (3) constantly innovate, (4) pay attention to changing market conditions and adjust, (5) build a robust data platform, and (6) ensure complete alignment on goals and incentives between the business and information technology departments.

Use Data Visualizations to Tell Stories and Gain Influence

- Research shows that the human brain can only deal with seven pieces of information at any one time and it's literally impossible for our brains to multi-task.

- As people reach information overload they start making stupid mistakes and bad choices because the brain region responsible for smart decision making has essentially left the premises.

- There are two challenges we have to deal with that require both hemispheres of our brains (1) Make important decisions quickly, based on lots of data and information, across many dimensions, and (2) We have to use data and information to create visualizations that lead to interesting insights.

- Visualizing data and complex relationships is our best bet to simplify things and tease out important insights. Critical insights that weren't visible when data was presented in tabular format were only made possible via visualizations.

- Infographics and visualizations are certainly very impressive, but acquiring the data, cleansing it and preparing it, takes up a bulk of the effort.

- The bottom line is that organizations have to invest in reducing the cost and effort required in the data preparation and cleansing steps.

- To become data-driven, start visualizing your data and use it to tell stories. You will become influential within your organization and gain immense credibility.

Winning with Data

- Organizations that wish to become data-driven must focus on achieving a high level of maturity in eleven knowledge areas related to data management. These are data architecture, data modeling and design, data storage and operations, data security, data integration and interoperability, documents and content, reference and master data, data warehousing and business intelligence, metadata, data quality, and data governance.

- In addition to the knowledge areas, there are several environmental elements, such as organization and culture (people), roles and responsibilities (people), activities (process), practices and techniques (process), deliverables (technology), and tools (technology), which are involved in a data management program and must be addressed.

- Leaders and data practitioners must be familiar with the most common data management terms in order to effectively communicate with each other.

- Data governance has become a top priority in the industry lately, due to a renewed focus on big data, data security, data privacy, master data management (MDM), reference data management, regulatory compliance, and data quality management. Many companies have some form of data governance in place, via data controls (e.g., SOX controls), structured development lifecycle (SDLC) checkpoints, design and code review boards, and architecture. However, these data controls and governance activities tend to lie within business silos and may not be handled consistently across all lines of business (LOB). Governing data across an enterprise in a standard and consistent manner is nontrivial, and companies frequently attempt it a few times before they get it right.

- Metadata is probably the most important concept in data management. But it is also the most misunderstood concept and therefore not given the importance it deserves.

- Given the importance of data for businesses, "Data Quality is Job 1" should be considered as a guiding principle or motto so that data quality gets woven into their DNA.

- Reference data management is closely related to and is a prerequisite for successfully implementing master data management (MDM). In fact, companies implementing MDM are forced to address RDM, to ensure that they are able to get the master data records right.

- MDM represents a single point of reference for important data, such as customers, employees, products, vendors, accounts, and so on.

- Big data refers to a capability that enables organizations to process very large amounts of data in a cost-effective manner. This capability is being utilized by organizations to gain deeper insights, get answers to complex questions, run predictive analytics, utilize machine learning, and leverage other capabilities to drive sales, marketing, planning, and R&D.

- IOT stands for Internet of Things. New devices or things such as wearables are being embedded within technology that gives them the ability to instantaneously send and receive data over the Internet without human or computer intervention. These things are connected to, and communicate via, the Internet and therefore can be controlled remotely, share data with other devices in real time, and have some level of intelligence built-in.

  Organizations that capture and process IOT-generated data gain deeper insights into the operating status of the device, the behavior of the user, or the sequence of events that have occurred in order to troubleshoot issues. IOT data can be combined with location data to gain even more insights.

Roadmap for Success

+ Before embarking on a journey, one needs a roadmap, a navigation system, and an acute awareness of the surroundings.

+ The first step in the journey is to conduct a data management maturity assessment. This will highlight the strengths and weaknesses of an organization's maturity, identify areas for improvement, and can be used as a guide while developing a roadmap for achieving the desired level of maturity and sophistication.

Making a Case for Change

+ Leaders have a tendency to focus on the analytical, not on the emotional drivers for change.

+ Senior leaders can influence the change, create a positive environment, and make the journey easier. They should use the core strengths of the organization and what it's done well in the past as impetuses for change.

+ Too much choice is paralyzing. Especially in a change situation, a big part of freeing up the creativity needed for change may be simplifying internal processes.

+ Change programs will hit roadblocks, so there should be time and resources allocated during the execution phase to deal with them.

- ◆ Senior leaders should use their power to guide the change and provide the necessary sponsorship to remove any impediments to change.

Glossary

Common Terms Used in Data Management

Leaders and data practitioners must be familiar with the most common data management terms to effectively communicate with one another.

There are many definitions for a particular term. I researched multiple sources and picked definitions that I felt best described a term.

Advanced Analytics: Analytics is the discovery and communication of meaningful patterns in data. Especially valuable in areas rich with recorded information, analytics relies on the simultaneous application of statistics, computer programming, and operations research to quantify performance. Analytics often favors data visualization to communicate insights. The end result might be a report, an indication of status, or an action taken automatically based on the information received.

Organizations may commonly apply analytics to business data, to describe, predict, and improve business performance. Specifically, areas within analytics include predictive analytics, enterprise decision management, retail analytics, store assortment and stock-keeping unit optimization, marketing optimization and marketing mix modeling, web analytics, sales force sizing and optimization, price and promotion modelling, predictive science, credit risk analysis, and fraud analytics.

Since analytics can require extensive computation (see big data), the algorithms and software used for analytics harness the most current methods in computer science, statistics, and mathematics.

Analytics Platform: Software or software and hardware that provides the tools and computational power needed to build and perform many different analytical queries.

Big Data: This term has been defined in many ways, but along similar lines. Doug Laney, then an analyst at the META Group, first defined big data in a 2001 report called "3-D Data Management: Controlling Data Volume, Velocity and Variety." Volume refers to the sheer size of the datasets. The McKinsey report, "Big Data: The Next Frontier for Innovation, Competition, and Productivity," expands on the volume aspect by saying that, 'Big Data' refers to datasets whose size is beyond the ability of typical database software tools to capture, store, manage, and analyze." Velocity refers to the speed at which the data is acquired and used. Not only are companies and organizations collecting more and more data at a faster rate, but they want to derive meaning from that data as soon as possible, often in real time. Variety refers to the different types of data that are available to collect and analyze in addition to the structured data found in a typical database.

Biometrics: The use of technology to identify people by one or more of their physical traits.

Business Intelligence: Business intelligence refers to an environment in which business users receive data that is reliable, consistent, understandable, easily manipulated, and timely. With this data, business users are able to conduct analyses that yield overall understanding of where the business has been, where it is now and where it will be in the near future. Business intelligence serves two main purposes. It monitors the financial and operational health of the organization (reports, alerts, alarms, analysis tools, key performance indicators, and dashboards). It also regulates the operation of the organization providing two-way integration with operational systems and information feedback analysis.

Cloud: A broad term that refers to any Internet-based application or service that is hosted remotely.

Complex Event Processing (CEP): CEP is the process of monitoring and analyzing all events across an organization's systems and acting on them when necessary in real time.

Crowdsourcing: The act of submitting a task or problem to the public for completion or solution.

Customer Relationship Management (CRM): Software that helps businesses manage sales and customer service processes.

Data Architecture: How enterprise data is structured. The actual structure or design varies depending on the eventual end result required. Data architecture has three stages or processes: conceptual representation of business entities, the logical representation of the relationships among those entities, and the physical construction of the system to support the functionality.

Data Custodian: The individual assigned the responsibility of operating systems, data centers, data warehouses, operational databases, and business operations in conformance with the policies and practices prescribed by the data owner.

Data Dictionary: A database about data and database structures. A catalog of all data elements, containing their names, structures, and information about their usage. A central location for metadata. Normally, data dictionaries are designed to store a limited set of available metadata, concentrating on the information relating to the data elements, databases, files, and programs of implemented systems.

Data and Information Governance: The exercise of decision-making and authority for data-related matters. The organizational bodies, rules, decision rights, and accountabilities of people and information systems as they perform information-related processes. Data and information governance determines how an organization makes decisions - how we "decide how to decide."

Data Model: A logical map that represents the inherent properties of the data independent of software, hardware, or machine performance considerations. The model shows data elements grouped into records, as well as the association around those records.

Data Privacy: The assurance that a person's or organization's personal and private information is not inappropriately disclosed. Ensuring data privacy requires access management, security, and other data protection efforts.

Data Profiling: The process of collecting statistics and information about data in an existing source. Data profiling, a critical first step in data migration, automates the identification of problematic data and metadata and enables companies to correct inconsistencies, redundancies, and inaccuracies in corporate databases.

Data Science: Data science is the extraction of knowledge from large volumes of data that are structured or unstructured, which is a continuation of the fields of Data Mining and Predictive Analytics, also known as knowledge discovery and data mining (KDD). Unstructured data can include emails, videos, photos, social media, and other user-generated content. Data science often requires sorting through a great amount of information and writing algorithms to extract insights from this data.

Data science employs techniques and theories drawn from many fields within the broad areas of mathematics, statistics, chemo metrics, information theory and computer science, including signal processing, probability models, machine learning, statistical learning, data mining, database, data engineering, pattern recognition and learning, visualization, predictive analytics, uncertainty modelling, data warehousing, data compression, computer programming, and high performance computing.

Methods that scale to big data are of particular interest in data science, although the discipline is not generally considered to be restricted to such data. The development of machine learning, a branch of artificial intelligence used to uncover patterns in data from which predictive models can be developed, has enhanced the growth and importance of data science.

Data and Information Security: The practice of protecting data and information from destruction or unauthorized access.

Data Quality: The measure of data to determine its worthiness for decision making, planning, or operations.

Data Steward: A data steward is a person responsible for the management of data elements (also known as critical data elements) - both the content and metadata. Data stewards have a specialist role that incorporates processes, policies, guidelines, and responsibilities for administering organizations' entire data in compliance with policy and/or regulatory obligations. A data steward may share some responsibilities with a data custodian. The primary responsibility of a data steward is to provide operation team members data entry rules for entering each data element into a computer.

Data Element: Describes the value found in each field in a table. Every field or column in a database table represents a single attribute of that table. An attribute is what the data in that field represents, while the value is the actual data that a specific field contains.

Data Integration: Data integration involves combining data residing in different sources and providing users with a unified view of these data. This process becomes significant in a variety of situations, which include both commercial (when two similar companies need to merge their databases) and scientific (combining research results from different bioinformatics repositories, for example) domains. Data integration appears with increasing frequency as the volume and the need to share existing data explodes. It has become the focus of extensive theoretical work, and numerous open problems remain unsolved.

Database Management: 1) A collection of all the data needed by a person or organization to perform their required functions. 2) A collection of related files or tables. 3) Any collection of data organized to answer queries; or, 4) [informally] a database management system. Databases usually consist of both data and metadata [data about the database's data]. When a database contains a description of its own structure, it is said to be self-describing. A database is integrated when it includes its relationships among data items as well as the data items themselves.

Data Migration: The process of transferring data between storage types, formats, or computer systems. Data migration is usually performed programmatically to achieve an automated migration, freeing up human resources from tedious tasks. It is required when organizations or individuals change computer systems or upgrade to new systems, or when systems merge (such as when the organizations that use them undergo a merger or takeover). To achieve an effective data migration procedure, data on the old system is mapped to the new system providing a design for data extraction and data loading. The design relates old data formats to the new system's formats and requirements. Programmatic data migration may involve many phases but it minimally includes data extraction where data is read from the old system and data loading where data is written to the new system.

Data Transformation: Creating "information" from data. This includes decoding production data and merging of records from multiple DBMS formats. It is also known as data scrubbing or data cleansing.

Data Type: Every field in every table in a database must be declared as a specific type of data with defined parameters and limitations (e.g., numeric, character or text, date, logical, etc.), known as a data type.

Data Virtualization: The process of abstracting different data sources through a single data access layer.

Data Visualization: Data visualization is viewed by many disciplines as a modern equivalent of visual communication. It is not owned by any one field, but rather finds interpretation across many (e.g., it is viewed as a modern branch of descriptive statistics by some, but also as a grounded theory development tool by others). It involves the creation and study of the visual representation of data, meaning "information that has been abstracted in some schematic form, including attributes or variables for the units of information."

De-identification: The act of removing all data that links a person to a particular piece of information.

Hadoop: An open source software library project administered by the Apache Software Foundation. Apache defines Hadoop as "a framework that allows for the distributed processing of large data sets across clusters of computers using a simple programming model."

Index: 1) A method used to reorder display or output records in a specific order, and 2) A data structure of pointers used to provide rapid, random access to rows in the table.

Integrity: The property of the database that ensures that the data contained in the database is as accurate and consistent as possible.

Internet-of-Things (IOT): IOT is the network of physical objects that contain embedded technology to communicate and sense or interact with their internal states or the external environment.

Key: A key is a field, or combination of fields, that uniquely identifies a record in a table.

Master Data Management: Master data management (MDM) is a comprehensive method of enabling an enterprise to link all of its critical data to one file, called a master file, that provides a common point of reference. When properly done, master data management streamlines data sharing among personnel and departments. In addition, master data management can facilitate computing in multiple system architectures, platforms, and applications.

Metadata Management: The definition and scope of metadata depends upon context. In the context of information management, metadata is generally thought of as providing information (what database stores it? what data type is it? how long is the field? etc.) about a data element. Within the context of data governance, the term also includes "business" metadata such as the names and roles of data stewards. Metadata repositories are employed to store and report on metadata.

NoSQL: A class of database management system that does not use the relational model. NoSQL is designed to handle large data volumes that do not follow a fixed schema. It is ideally suited for use with very large data volumes that do not require the relational mode.

Parsing: Intelligently separating a field value or string into its component parts (e.g., parsing a full name into its five characteristic components: prefix, first name, middle name [or initial], last name and suffix). The opposite action is called concatenation.

Predictive Analytics: Using statistical functions on one or more datasets to predict trends or future events.

Predictive Modelling: The process of developing a model that will most likely predict a trend or outcome.

Query: A (usually) complex SELECT statement for decision support.

Records: Synonymous with row and tuple. An instance of data in a table, a record is a collection of all the facts related to one physical or conceptual entity; often referring to a single object or person, usually represented as a row of data in a table, and sometimes referred to as a tuple in some, particularly older, database management systems.

Reference Data Management: Reference data is data that defines the set of permissible values to be used by other data fields. Reference data gains in value when it is widely re-used and widely referenced. Typically, it does not change overly much in terms of definition (apart from occasional revisions). Reference data often is defined by standards organizations (such as country codes as defined in ISO 3166-1).

Reports: An automated business process or related functionality that provides a detailed, formal account of relevant or requested information.

Risk Management: In a broad sense, to assess, minimize, and prevent negative consequences posed by a potential threat. The term "risk management" has significantly different meanings that can affect data governance programs. At an enterprise level, "risk" refers to many types of risk (operational, financial, compliance, etc.); managing risk is a key responsibility of corporate boards and executive teams. Within financial institutions (or in the context of a GRC program), risk management may be a boundary-spanning department that focuses on risk to investments, loans, or mortgages. At a project level, "risk management" is an effort that should be undertaken as part of project management, focusing on risks to the successful completion of the project. From a compliance/auditing/controls perspective, "risk assessments" and "risk management" are high-effort activities included in the COSO, and COBIT frameworks and required by Sarbanes-Oxley and other compliance efforts. Data governance programs may be asked to support any of these risk management efforts, and may need input from these efforts to resolve data-related issues.

Sensitive Data: Data that is private, personal, or proprietary and must be protected from unauthorized access.

SQL: Pronounced "Sequel", it stands for "structured query language," the standard format for commands that most database software understands. There are different dialects, since every program handles certain types of data differently, but the core commands are always the same. ODBC uses SQL as the "Lingua Franca" to transfer information between databases. Currently accepted ANSI standard is SQL-92.

Strategic Data Management: (1) A concept – referring to the ability of an organization to precisely define, easily integrate, and effectively retrieve data for both internal applications and external communication, and (2) A business objective – focused on the creation of accurate, consistent, and transparent content. SDM emphasizes data precision, granularity, and meaning and is concerned with how the content is integrated into business applications as well as how it is passed along from one business process to another. SDM requires a strategic approach to choosing the right processes, technologies, and resources (i.e., data owners, governance, stewardship, data analysts, and data architects). SDM is a challenge for organizations because it requires alignment among multiple stakeholders (including IT, operations, finance, strategy and end users) and relates to an area (creation and use of common data) that has not traditionally had a clear "owner."

Validation: Verification that a field's value doesn't violate any constraints defined for it by the database or file structure.

Data Visualization Tools To Explore

A few visualization tools you may want to explore are listed below. Each has its unique strengths, so you will have to evaluate them individually, based on your specific requirements *(Note: This is not meant as an endorsement of any product and is not a comprehensive list):*

VibrantData (vibrantdata.io): A network data visualization tool used to discover hidden relationships across people, topics or projects.

Tableau (www.tableau.com): Provides self-service data visualisation and analysis.

Qlik (www.qlik.com): Provides self-service data visualisation and analysis.

D3.js (www.d3js.org/): D3.js is a JavaScript library that uses HTML, SVG, and CSS to render some amazing diagrams and charts from a variety of data sources.

Raw (raw.densitydesign.org/): Raw defines itself as 'the missing link between spreadsheets and vector graphics'. It is built on top of D3.js and is extremely well designed. It has such an intuitive interface that you'll feel like you've used it before. It is open-source and doesn't require any registration.

Leaflet (leafletjs.com/): Leaflet makes it easy to use OpenStreetMap data and integrate fully interactive data visualisation in an HTML5/CSS3 wrapper.

Exhibit (www.simile-widgets.org/exhibit/): Developed at MIT. Exhibit makes it easy to create interactive maps, and other data-based visualizations that are orientated towards teaching or static/historical based data sets, such as flags pinned to countries, or birth-places of famous people.

Wolfram-Alpha (www.wolframalpha.com/): Billed as a "computational knowledge engine", the Google rival WolframAlpha is really good at intelligently displaying charts in response to data queries without the need for any configuration.

Visual.ly (create.visual.ly/): Visual.ly is a combined gallery and infographic generation tool. It offers a simple toolset for building stunning data representations, as well as a platform to share your creations.

FusionCharts (www.fusioncharts.com/): FusionCharts Suite XT brings you 90+ charts and gauges, 965 data-driven maps, and ready-made business dashboards and demos.

Many Eyes (www-01.ibm.com/software/analytics/many-eyes/): Developed by IBM, Many Eyes allows you to quickly build visualizations from publically available or uploaded data sets, and features a wide range of analysis types including the ability to scan text for keyword density and saturation.

Google Charts (developers.google.com/chart/interactive/docs/): The seminal charting solution for much of the web, Google Charts is highly flexible and has an excellent set of developer tools behind it.

R (www.r-project.org/): How many other pieces of software have an entire search engine dedicated to them? A statistical package used to parse large data sets, R is a very complex tool, and one that takes a while to understand, but has a strong community and package library, with more and more being produced.

Gephi (gephi.github.io/): When people talk about relatedness, social graphs and co-relations, they are really talking about how two nodes are related to one another relative to the other nodes in a network. The nodes in question could be people in a company, words in a document or passes in a football game, but the math's the same.

Notes

Chapter 1

1. *CISCO Systems* white paper, "The Zettabyte Era – Trends and Analysis," June 2015, http://www.cisco.com/c/en/us/solutions/collateral/service-provider/visual-networking-index-vni/VNI_Hyperconnectivity_WP.html

2. *Computerworld* article, "World's Data Will Grow by 50X in next decade, IDC Study Predicts," June 2011, http://www.computerworld.com/article/2509588/data-center/world-s-data-will-grow-by-50x-in-next-decade--idc-study-predicts.html

3. *Quartz* article, "More People Around the World have Cell Phones than ever had Land Lines," February 2014, http://torcyclistonline.tv/feature/decoding-bearings-and-oil-seals-mc-garage.html

4. *IDC report* titled "Digital Universe of Opportunities: Rich Data and the Increasing Value of the Internet of Things," April 2014, http://www.emc.com/leadership/digital-universe/2014iview/executive-summary.htm

5. *McKinsey and Company Report,* "Big Data: The Next Frontier for Innovation, competition, and productivity," published in May 2011, http://www.mckinsey.com/business-functions/business-technology/our-insights/big-data-the-next-frontier-for-innovation

6. Blog post by Dylan Tweney that discussed mobile Internet related predictions by Digi Capital published February 20, 2015, http://www.notey.com/@venturebeat_unofficial/external/3608370/mobile-growth-is-huge-and-could-surge-at-least-3x-in-the-next-two-years.html

7. Article in *Popular Science,* "Your full genome can be sequenced and analyzed for just $1,000," published September 30, 2015, http://www.popsci.com/cost-full-genome-sequencing-drops-to-1000

8. Data Journalism Handbook, http://datajournalismhandbook.org/1.0/en/index.html

Chapter 2

1. The Johari Window, https://en.wikipedia.org/wiki/Johari_window

Chapter 3

1. Amar, A.D., and Hlupic, V., (2012), "Synthesizing Knowledge to develop Leadership for Managing in Knowledge Organizations," presented at the Academy of Management Conference, Boston 1-7, August 2012.

Chapter 4

1. *IBM blog* post by Sushil Pramanick, "Analytics ROI – Strategy to Execution," published on January 7, 2013, http://www.ibmbigdatahub.com/blog/analytics-roi-strategy-execution

2. Blog post by Stan Przybylinski, "Integration is still the major challenge in PLM adoption," published on November 30, 2014, http://beyondplm.com/2014/11/30/integration-is-still-the-major-challenge-in-plm-adoption/

3. Unified Data Architecture by Teradata, http://www.teradata.com/solutions-and-industries/unified-data-architecture/

4. Blog post by Antons Matrosovs, "Visiting Gartner Summit 2015 in London," published on July 23, 2015, http://blog.ideaportriga.com/visiting-gartner-summit-2015-in-london/

5. *McKinsey and Company report*, "Big Data: The Next Frontier for Innovation, competition, and productivity," published in May 2011, http://www.mckinsey.com/business-functions/business-technology/our-insights/big-data-the-next-frontier-for-innovation

Chapter 5

1. IBM Cognitive Colloquium Spotlights Uncovering Dark Data, October, 2015, http://www.informationweek.com/cloud/software-as-a-service/ibm-cognitive-colloquium-spotlights-uncovering-dark-data/d/d-id/1322647

Chapter 6

1. Computer Weekly, "Data set to grow 10-fold by 2020 as internet of things takes off," April 2014, http://www.computerweekly.com/news/2240217788/Data-set-to-grow-10-fold-by-2020-as-internet-of-things-takes-off

Chapter 7

1. Bloomberg, "Missed Alarms and 40 Million Stolen Credit Card Numbers: How Target Blew It," March, 2014, http://www.bloomberg.com/news/articles/2014-03-13/target-missed-warnings-in-epic-hack-of-credit-card-data

2. The Data Warehousing Institute Report, "Data Quality and the Bottom Line – Achieving Business Success through a commitment to High Quality Data," 2002, http://download.101com.com/pub/tdwi/Files/DQReport.pdf

3. Blog post by Jim Harris, "The Data Quality Wager," April 2011, http://www.ocdqblog.com/home/the-data-quality-wager.html?rq=15%20to%2045%25

4. Katherine Barrett and Richard Greene, "The Causes, Costs, and Consequences of Bad Government Data," June 2015, http://www.governing.com/topics/mgmt/gov-bad-data.html

Chapter 8

1. Ford Commercial - "Quality is Job No. 1," 1984, https://www.youtube.com/watch?v=xZISPbKgbvw

2. Auto Industry Bailout (GM, Ford, Chrysler), May 2016, http://useconomy.about.com/od/criticalissues/a/auto_bailout.htm

3. *Quality Digest,* "Making Quality Job 1 Again," http://www.quality-digest.com/sept01/html/ford.html

4. Inflation Calculator, http://www.saving.org/inflation/inflation.php?amount=300

Chapter 9

1. Infinitive Digital BrainFest 2015 Panel Discussion, "The Dark Side of Big Data: What Happens When It Falls into the Wrong Hands and Why Regulators Are So Interested," May 2016, http://brainfest.infinitive.com/session-items/dark-side-big-data-happens-falls-wrong-hands-regulators-interested/

2. Definition of *Garbage In, Garbage Out,* https://www.techopedia.com/definition/3801/garbage-in-garbage-out-gigo

Chapter 10

1. Chartered Global Management Accountant (CGMA) Report, "Joining the Dots – Decision Making for a new Era," 2016, http://www.cgma.org/Resources/Pages/Joiningthedots.aspx

2. Forbes article, "Inside American Express' Big Data Journey," April 2016, http://www.forbes.com/sites/ciocentral/2016/04/27/inside-american-express-big-data-journey/#652b3028127f

Chapter 11

1. Satya Nadella Microsoft Keynote in New York City, "Data is the new Electricity," March 2016, https://www.microsoft.com/en-us/server-cloud/data-driven.aspx.

2. Klaus Schwab, "The Fourth Industrial Revolution," Kindle Edition, January 2016, World Economic Forum, https://www.amazon.com/Fourth-Industrial-Revolution-Klaus-Schwab-ebook/dp/B01AIT6SZ8?ie=UTF8&*Version*=1&*entries*=0

Chapter 12

1. Definition of "Politics," https://en.wikipedia.org/wiki/Politics

2. PriceWaterhouseCoopers LLC Report, "Great Expectations: The evolution of the chief data officer," February 2015, https://www.pwc.com/us/en/financial-services/publications/viewpoints/assets/pwc-chief-data-officer-cdo.pdf

Chapter 13

1. Forbes article, "A Very Brief History of Big Data," May 2013, http://www.forbes.com/sites/gilpress/2013/05/09/a-very-short-history-of-big-data/#4eae7efd55da

2. Forbes article, "A Simple Explanation of Internet of Things," May 2014, http://www.forbes.com/sites/jacobmorgan/2014/05/13/simple-explanation-internet-things-that-anyone-can-understand/#73b0306e6828

Chapter 15

1. Nextgov.com article, "Agency Data Chiefs on the Move," September 2015, http://www.nextgov.com/big-data/2015/09/agency-data-chiefs-move-some-out-government/121637/

2. IBM Center for Applied Insights, "Stories from Data Leaders," July 2015, http://www.ibm.com/smarterplanet/us/en/centerforappliedinsights/article/cdo_insights.html

3. Encyclopedia Britannica, "The Financial Crisis of 2008 – A Year in Review 2008," 2008, http://www.britannica.com/topic/Financial-Crisis-of-2008-The-1484264

4. Morrison and Foerster Report, "Dodd-Frank – A Primer," 2010, http://media.mofo.com/files/Uploads/Images/Summary-DoddFrankAct.pdf

5. European Commission Rules - Solvency II, May 2016, http://ec.europa.eu/finance/insurance/solvency/solvency2/index_en.htm

6. Basel Committee of Banking Supervision (BCBS) – BASEL Regulations, http://www.bis.org/bcbs/basel3.htm?m=3%7C14%7C572

Chapter 17

1. John Gray, "Men are from Mars, Women are from Venus - A Practical Guide for Improving Communication and Getting What You Want in Your Relationships," 1993, http://anakkusayang.com/Download/ladies.pdf

Chapter 18

1. Carl Anderson, "Creating a Data-Driven Organization – Practical Advice from the Trenches," July 2015, O'Reilly Media, http://shop. oreilly.com/product/0636920035848.do#tab_04_2

2. Wired magazine, "How Do You Define Startup Culture," http://www. wired.com/insights/2013/09/how-do-you-define-startup-culture/

3. Sridhar Balasubramaniam, "Insight Into Innovation – Why Companies Must Innovate," March 2013, http://www.kenan-flagler.unc.edu/ news/2013/03/why-companies-must-innovate

4. Project Management Institute Report, "Organizational Agility," http://www.pmi.org/~/media/PDF/Research/Organizational-Agility-In-Depth-Report.ashx

5. Microsoft Data Platform, https://partner.microsoft.com/en-US/ membership/data-platform-competency

Chapter 19

1. *Newsweek* article by Sharon Begley, "The Science of Making Decisions," February 2011, http://www.newsweek.com/ science-making-decisions-68627

2. Blog post by Belle Beth Cooper, "10 Surprising Facts About How Our Brain Works," December 2013, https://blog.bufferapp. com/10-surprising-facts-about-how-our-brain-works

3. Martin Grandjean, "The Top-Secret U.S. Intelligence 'Black Budget'," August 2013, http://www.martingrandjean.ch/ data-visualization-top-secret-us-intelligence-budget/

4. Cliff Kuang, "The Insane Choices You Face At The Drugstore," November 2011, http://www.fastcodesign.com/1665355/ infographic-of-the-day-the-insane-choices-you-face-at-the-drugstore

5. TED talk by David McCandless, "The Beauty of Data Visualization," July 2010, http://www.ted.com/talks/ david_mccandless_the_beauty_of_data_visualization

6. TED talk by JoAnn Kuchera-Morin, "Stunning Data Visualizations in the AlloSphere," February 2009, http://www.ted.com/talks/ joann_kuchera_morin_tours_the_allosphere

Chapter 20

1. DAMA Data Management Book of Knowledge, 11 Knowledge Areas, https://www.dama.org/content/body-knowledge

2. DAMA Data Management Book of Knowledge (DMBOK) 7 Environmental Elements, http://www.damaindiana.org/Presentations/DAMA%20Indiana%20Data%20Architecture%20Management.pdf

Chapter 21

1. CIO magazine, "Demystifying Master Data Management," April 2007, http://www.cio.com/article/2439152/data-management/demystifying-master-data-management.html

2. The Data Governance Institute, "Defining Data Governance," http://www.datagovernance.com/defining-data-governance/

3. Sarbanes Oxley Law (SOX), https://en.wikipedia.org/wiki/Sarbanes–Oxley_Act

4. System Development Life Cycle (SDLC), https://en.wikipedia.org/wiki/Systems_development_life_cycle

Chapter 22

1. Brad Feld blog post, "Three Magic Numbers," February, 2012, http://www.feld.com/archives/2012/02/three-magic-numbers.html

2. Robert Scoble and Shel Israel,"Age of Context," September 2013, http://www.amazon.com/gp/product/1492348430/ref=as_li_ss_tl?ie=UTF8&camp=1789&creative=390957&creativeASIN=1492348430&linkCode=as2&tag=teco07-20

Chapter 23

1. Use of Metadata by NSA, "Former CIA Director – We Kill People Based on Metadata," May 2014, https://www.rt.com/usa/158460-cia-director-metadata-kill-people/

2. CNN Money Report, "Obama and NSA - So What is Metadata Anyway?" January 2014, http://money.cnn.com/2014/01/17/technology/security/obama-metadata-nsa/

3. Description of a Metadata Repository, https://en.wikipedia.org/wiki/Metadata_repository

Chapter 24

1. CrowdFlower Company, https://en.wikipedia.org/wiki/CrowdFlower

2. J.M. Juran, "Quality Management Thinker," http://mbsportal.bl.uk/taster/subjareas/busmanhist/mgmtthinkers/juran.aspx

Chapter 27

1. Forbes article, "A Very Short History of Big Data," May 2013, http://www.forbes.com/sites/gilpress/2013/05/09/a-very-short-history-of-big-data

2. Apache Hadoop Project, "What is Apache Hadoop," http://hadoop.apache.org/

3. Forbes article, "Gartner's Big Data Definition Consists of 3 Parts, Not To Be Confused With Three 'V's," March 2013, http://www.forbes.com/sites/gartnergroup/2013/03/27/gartners-big-data-definition-consists-of-three-parts-not-to-be-confused-with-three-vs/#3257628c3bf6

Chapter 28

1. McKinsey Quarterly article by Michael Chu, Markus Loffler, and Roger Roberts, "The Internet of Things," March 2010, http://www.mckinsey.com/industries/high-tech/our-insights/the-internet-of-things

Chapter 29

1. CMMI Institute, "Data Management Maturity," http://cmmiinstitute.com/data-management-maturity

2. Carnegie Mellon University's Software Engineering Institute site, http://www.sei.cmu.edu/

Chapter 30

1. Harvard Business Review article by Michael D. Watkins, "What is Organizational Culture Change? And Why Should We Care?," May 2013, https://hbr.org/2013/05/what-is-organizational-culture

2. Harvard Business Review article by Jay Lorsch and Emily McTague, "Culture Is Not the Culprit," April 2016, https://hbr.org/2016/04/culture-is-not-the-culprit

3. Chip Heath Profile, https://www.gsb.stanford.edu/faculty-research/faculty/chip-heath

4. Chip Health and Dan Heath, "Switch: How to Change Things When Change Is Hard," February 2010, http://www.amazon.com/Switch-Change-Things-When-Hard/dp/0385528752/ref=sr_1_1?ie=UTF8&qid=1465228005&sr=8-1&keywords=switch+dan+heath

5. Computerworld article by Jonny Evans, "The Untold Story behind Apple's 'Think Different' campaign," June 2015, http://www.computerworld.com/article/2936344/apple-mac/the-untold-story-behind-apple-s-think-different-campaign.html

Conclusion

1. Klaus Schwab, "The Fourth Industrial Revolution: what it means, how to respond," January 2016, https://www.weforum.org/agenda/2016/01/the-fourth-industrial-revolution-what-it-means-and-how-to-respond/

2. Spencer Stuart study, "Chief Marketing Officer Tenure Climbs to 48 Months," March 2015, https://www.spencerstuart.com/who-we-are/media-center/chief-marketing-officer-tenure-climbs-to-48-months

Index

A

Accountability 74, 113, 146, 155
Agile execution 125
Airbnb 27
Alan Mulally 186
Alation 175
Alteryx 175
Amazon 27
American Express 81
AMEX 81
Anne Neuberger 71
appetite for change 82
Apple 27, 34, 35, 189
Aristotle 185
Ash Gupta 81
Automation 156

B

Bad data 60, 63, 64
Barnes & Noble 28
benchmarking 164
Big Data xx, xxi, 30, 31, 34, 45, 46,
    47, 48, 50, 52, 67, 71, 73, 74,
    75, 76, 78, 79, 80, 81, 82, 83,
    87, 93, 95, 109, 143, 159, 162,
    164, 173, 174, 175, 176, 191,
    200, 201, 202, 206, 209, 210,
    213
Big Data stack 80
Biometrics 210
Birst 175
Blockbuster 28
Borders 28
Brad Feld 158
Business Intelligence 210

C

CDO 92, 93, 95, 96, 99, 100, 102,
    103, 104, 105, 106, 107, 108,
    109, 110
Center for Neural Decision Making
    129
Centers for Disease Control (CDC)
    73
CEO 42, 45, 60, 66, 70, 71, 92, 96, 99,
    108, 164, 166, 167
CFO 92, 95, 96, 99, 108
Change Management 154
Change programs 188
Chip Heath 187
Ciba-Geigy 186
CIO 54, 56, 60, 92, 95, 96, 99, 103,
    104, 106, 108, 110
Circuit City 28
CISO 65, 71
Cloud 40, 49, 85, 91, 103, 108, 117,
    125, 211
Cloudera 175
CMO 95, 96
comScore 27
Context 75, 114, 158, 159, 192
Contextual data 162
Contextual Gap 80
COO 41, 92, 95, 96, 99, 108
Corporate Leadership 1.0 39, 40, 43
Corporate Leadership 2.0 39, 40, 43
critical success factors 188
CRO 71, 92, 95, 96, 99, 108
culture 184, 185, 186, 187, 193, 194,
    198, 230
Culture 154
Customer 171, 211
Cybersecurity 60, 65, 75, 236

About the Author

JAY ZAIDI is the founder and managing partner of AlyData www. alydata.com. As an entrepreneur, strategic advisor, and thought leader, he specializes in strategic data management, analytics, and change management. His firm provides services and solutions to help companies improve decision-making and performance, using data as a weapon of choice.

Jay founded AlyData in 2014. For the thirteen previous years, he led enterprise data management programs at Fannie Mae, and he spent seven years in management consulting at PriceWaterhouseCoopers LLC and other firms prior to that. At Fannie Mae, he directly reported to the chief data officer and led data quality, metadata, master data management, analytics, and business intelligence organizations. During his tenure there, he was instrumental in delivering ten major data initiatives across eight company divisions.

In 2012, Jay's team was awarded the Global Innovation Award for Fortifying Overall Operations with Global Data Quality by Informatica. He blogs on LinkedIn, is currently the most viewed author in the categories of data management and master data management on Quora, (www.quora.com/profile/Jay-Zaidi)and is a regular speaker at industry conferences.

In addition to his practical experience in strategic data management and cybersecurity, Jay has an M.S. in computer science from Texas A&M University and a bachelor's degree in electronics and communications engineering from Osmania University, India. He lives with his family outside Washington, DC, and is an avid photographer, an automobile enthusiast, loves to travel, and closely follows current events.

Learn more about Jay via his LinkedIn profile(https://www.linkedin.com/in/javedzaidi). Follow him on twitter @jayzaidi.

About Dr. Kirk Borne

DR. **KIRK BORNE** is the principal data scientist for Booz Allen Hamilton (since 2015) within the Next-Gen Analytics and Data Science account of the Strategic Innovation Group. He is an internationally recognized speaker, author, researcher, teacher, adviser, and thought leader in data science disciplines (databases, data mining, machine learning, modeling, statistics, data ethics, and data-driven applications). He has over thirty years of professional experience in roles associated with management, research, and discovery within large data systems. He earned a PhD in Astronomy at Caltech, and received a BS in Physics summa cum laude at Louisiana State University. He spent twelve years as professor of astrophysics and computational science at George Mason University (GMU) in the graduate and undergraduate data science programs. He was co-creator of the world's first data science BS degree program (at GMU). He advised seven completed PhD dissertations in data science, computational informatics, and astronomy. Before that, he worked eighteen years on various NASA contracts - as research scientist, as a manager on a large science data system contract, and as the Hubble Telescope Data Archive project scientist.

Kirk is a member of advisory boards for several firms in areas related to data science, analytics, and big data applications and services, and is on the editorial board of several journals related to informatics, data science, and computing. He has worked with numerous businesses (large and small) and federal agencies, where he has applied his expertise in science and large data systems as a consultant and adviser, focusing on the use of data for discovery, decision support, and innovation across many different domains and industries. He has contributed over two hundred conference talks worldwide, and has been an invited (and/or keynote) speaker for over two hundred additional events (conferences, meetups, universities, and organizations). He has published over two hundred papers (including more than sixty peer-reviewed publications). He is the originator of the field of Astroinformatics (data science for astronomy) and contributes to data science development within numerous organizations (public, private, federal, and nonprofit) to enhance data literacy and data science skills in the next-generation workforce.

Dr. Borne is also a blogger (rocketdatascience.org) and actively promotes data literacy for everyone by disseminating information related to data science and analytics on social media, where he has been named consistently since 2013 among the top worldwide influencers in big data and data science. In 2016, he was identified as the number-one worldwide influencer in big data, the number-two influencer in data science and machine learning, and a top-twenty influencer in the Internet of Things. You can follow him on Twitter at @KirkDBorne.

Your Notes

33821393R00137

Made in the USA
Middletown, DE
28 July 2016